Inquiry-Based Learning

Inquiry-Based Learning

Designing Instruction to Promote Higher Level Thinking

Third Edition

Teresa Coffman

ROWMAN & LITTLEFIELD
Lanham • Boulder • New York • London

Published by Rowman & Littlefield
A wholly owned subsidiary of The Rowman & Littlefield Publishing Group, Inc.
4501 Forbes Boulevard, Suite 200, Lanham, Maryland 20706
www.rowman.com

Unit A, Whitacre Mews, 26-34 Stannary Street, London SE11 4AB

Copyright © 2017 by Teresa Coffman

All rights reserved. No part of this book may be reproduced in any form or by any electronic or mechanical means, including information storage and retrieval systems, without written permission from the publisher, except by a reviewer who may quote passages in a review.

British Library Cataloguing in Publication Information Available

Library of Congress Cataloging-in-Publication Data is Available

ISBN 978-1-4758-2567-1 (cloth: alk. paper)
ISBN 978-1-4758-2568-8 (pbk: alk. paper)
ISBN 978-1-4758-2569-5 (electronic)

∞™ The paper used in this publication meets the minimum requirements of American National Standard for Information Sciences—Permanence of Paper for Printed Library Materials, ANSI/NISO Z39.48-1992.

Printed in the United States of America

Contents

Preface		vii
Acknowledgments		ix
1	Teaching with Inquiry: An Introduction	1
2	Teaching and Student Learning Using Inquiry	15
3	Integrating Computer Technologies as a Cognitive Tool	27
4	Technology Integration Models	37
5	Social Media and Collaboration	51
6	Digital Citizenship	61
7	Information Literacy	71
8	Engaging in Problem-Based Learning	81
9	Global Connections and Telecollaborative Learning	93
10	Using Technologies for Assessment and Feedback	107
11	Engaging Learners around Inquiry with Blended Learning	121
References		133
About the Author		139

Preface

As an instructor, teaching both graduate and undergraduate students in education, I have found that many textbooks in instructional technology do not focus enough on learning and instruction. Instead, they concentrate on a specific tool or even a particular skill that is only useful in limited circumstances. This third edition text provides a tripartite emphasis on learning, instruction, and technology integration thereby helping to fill this gap.

Examples used in this book are drawn from educational situations that help illustrate theoretical concepts important to learning and thinking more concretely about how to use digital technologies as a cognitive tool throughout instruction.

This book has an applied focus and encourages exploration of a variety of educational technologies. It also has a reflective emphasis encouraging practice and then reflection on how best to integrate technologies into classroom instruction.

The content in this third edition text has been updated from the past two editions to reflect the way educators currently view teaching and learning from an inquiry-based approach. Content has been added, removed, or reorganized to make it more relevant to practicing teachers today.

New to this third edition is a case scenario running throughout the book that helps to organize key features of the chapter content. Introduced in chapter 1 and presented at the beginning of chapters 2 through 11 to help explain the content more deeply, this scenario also provides an opportunity to think more directly about how information in the chapter applies to specific pedagogy, content, and technology needs.

End-of-chapter Reflections ask poignant questions for the reader to consider based on their overall classroom and integrating content-specific ideas. End-of-chapter Skill Building Activities push beyond the opening scenario to encourage the reader to think more creatively and incorporate digital tools that allow for more conceptual and applied learning.

Illustrations, examples, and activities all attempt to align what is being mastered through this text with how it applies to today's students, content knowledge and requirements for teaching and learning, and advancement of overall technology skills and knowledge.

I hope you enjoy this text and it serves as a welcome addition to your library of instructional resources that incorporate technology and inquiry to help develop and strengthen your body of knowledge. Enjoy!

Acknowledgments

As an instructor, I constantly challenge myself to improve my craft by seeking better ways to meet the needs of students in both teaching and learning. As part of this professional development, I have paid close attention to the comments and feedback from students over the years to help me improve my curriculum. As a result, I owe a very special thank you to each of my past, present, and future students for making me the educator I am today.

I also want to thank Dr. Mary Beth Klinger who provided thoughtful critique and helpful suggestions for improvement for this third edition text. I also want to thank the editors and reviewers at Rowman & Littlefield, Education Division for their support.

Finally, I would like to thank my readers who have asked questions and provided feedback to help guide improvements made in this current edition.

Chapter One

Teaching with Inquiry
An Introduction

Welcome to the world of inquiry learning! Defined by experience and exploration, it involves students in the process of learning through good questioning. From this, they acquire a deeper understanding of the material being taught. The inquiry-oriented learning approach implements a constructivist model that encourages students to interact with content around established learning goals.

Students make meaningful and thoughtful connections to the world around them by asking questions, conducting research, and formulating informed decisions using technology tools that are as authentic as the problem they are tackling. See the Inquiry Learning Design Framework in figure 1.1.

When designing an inquiry lesson, the goal is to find constructive ways to promote higher level thinking around course content by incorporating both structured and purposeful activities. These activities are often centered around an essential question and subsequent subquestions to guide student thinking and learning.

Questions should motivate or "hook" students and gain their interest. They also provide opportunities for students to investigate phenomenon from multiple perspectives and garner viewpoints individually, in small groups, and as a class.

WHAT IS INQUIRY?

Designing instruction with the purpose of stimulating inquiry requires a structured approach. The teacher scaffolds the learning process to engage students around curricular goals and authentic yet meaningful tasks so that connections can be made to essential questions.

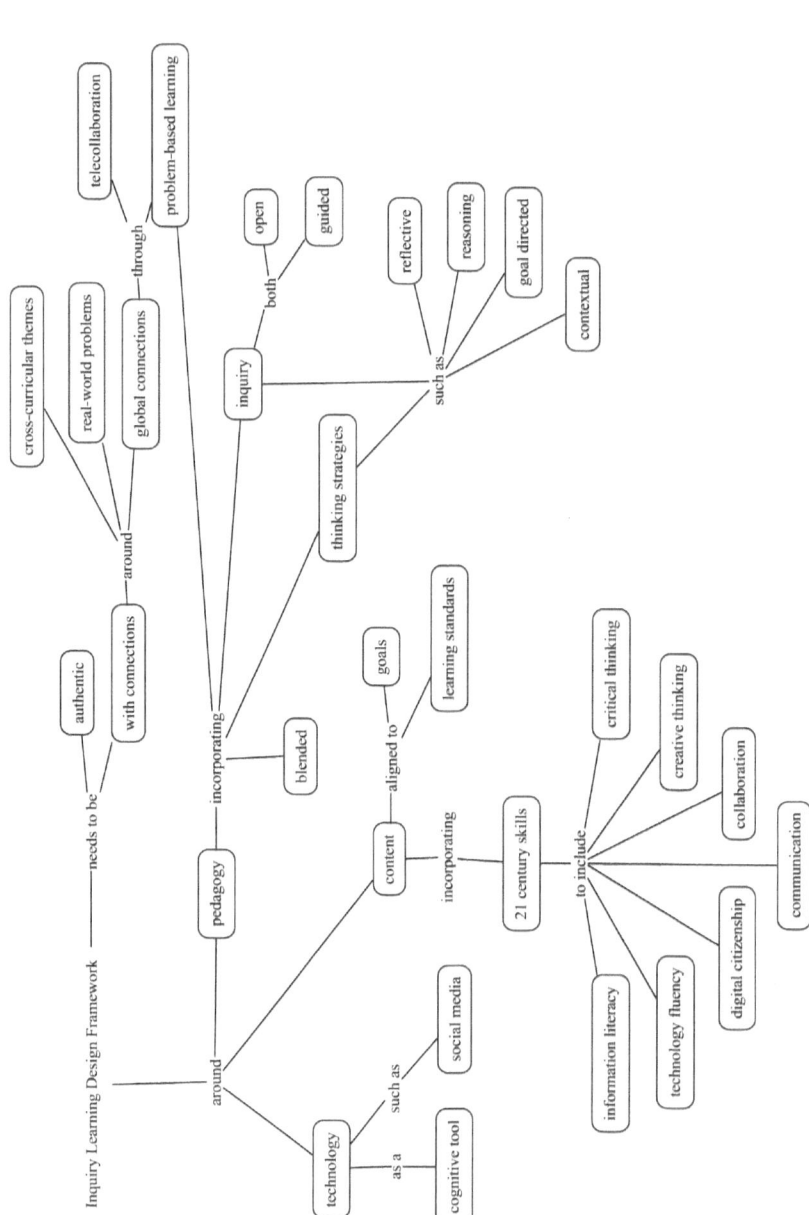

Figure 1.1. Inquiry Learning Design Framework

Digital technologies assist and elevate this process. As students interact in today's complex and global world, they interact with multiple technologies to retrieve information, compile it into a manageable product, and often redistribute it to a shared community.

This digital interaction with content and information, as well as with other people, has changed the way students interact and think about the world around them. As educators, we strive to capture this interconnectedness and incorporate it into teaching and student learning.

Inquiry-oriented learning builds upon students' natural curiosity of the world and embeds relevant real-world problems and issues into the curriculum. Posing thoughtful questions and providing quality resources help students answer essential questions. Infusing inquiry into your lessons is paramount for improving critical thinking and overall analysis.

Inquiry-oriented learning extends student knowledge and understanding. As the teacher, you encourage students to "think outside the box" and bring in outside interests to apply to their learning process. They work with other students or experts in the real world and beyond the classroom walls.

The goal in using inquiry is for students to learn the skills needed to think creatively in developing solutions and to come to a new understanding of information, data, and concepts that can then be shared with others to both learn from and build upon.

TWENTY-FIRST-CENTURY SKILLS AND THE INQUIRY PROCESS

The use of inquiry changes the way we think about learning and teaching. In the classroom, inquiry-oriented learning takes many forms. It involves moving away from a traditional teacher-centered approach and toward a more student-centered style. One that encourages students to take responsibility for their learning by thinking in more complex terms about the course content and how it fits into their world.

Students still gain a solid understanding of the foundational knowledge and skills required by the course content, but as the teacher, you begin to think differently about how you achieve this goal. Consider the essential understandings within your curriculum and how each relate to the world we live in. Next, identify essential questions and quality resources that will help students build both foundational knowledge and more complex thinking skills. You are teaching your students how to think as well as learn content.

As you develop and identify the essential question for your unit or lesson around your curriculum standards, also consider how to seamlessly integrate twenty-first-century skills into each lesson. How will you support students in gaining the necessary skills and knowledge to apply, analyze, synthesize, and evaluate information to create new knowledge and skills?

Within education, when we consider twenty-first-century skills and student preparation for the world outside of a school's traditional four walls, the emphasis is on developing creative thinkers and self-directed risk takers who ask thoughtful questions and seek good answers that go beyond mere surface understanding.

THEMES

The three main themes or ideas within this text include the following:

- Today's students are shaped by the numerous technologies that are available in this multifaceted, global environment.
- Integrating technology should not be treated as something separate or special. It represents a vast array of tools and strategies that can be integrated regularly and seamlessly into your teaching.
- Providing authentic and personal learning experiences designed around inquiry can be a valuable learning experience for students.

As you read through this book, think about how you can incorporate good teaching and inquiry throughout your curriculum in order to provide students with an active role in their learning process. Learning goals are identified, but students are also being prepared to think at more complex levels by seamlessly integrating authentic problems, resources, and digital tools.

Students need to be taught specific skills and strategies to think more deeply. Careful planning of activities and inquiry lessons will help them develop these skills. One way to do this is to think differently about your curriculum. Identify how your course standards relate to the larger context and real-world essentials. Then, identify essential questions that hook or gain the interest of your students. Essential questions are not answerable; instead their purpose is to stimulate thought, provoke inquiry, and motivate students by inspiring even more thoughtful questions.

As you review your learning standards and think about your curriculum, what are the essential questions that your curriculum is attempting to answer? Consider how you can incorporate these questions into your instruction.

Essential questions surround each content area without exception. It may be a challenge for you to discover them, but they are there. The process of designing a good inquiry lesson can often be a bit messy as it demands a new way to think about your own teaching as well as your students' learning. But the results are rewarding for both you and your students.

As you venture forth, it is important to remember that many of your students have been taught in similar ways as you have: the teacher at the center guiding learning with an expected right or wrong answer. There has been little to no inclusion of the outside world or even integration of other subjects being taught throughout the school curriculum. Traditionally and historically, there has been a disconnect in the way we educate our students.

In this new approach, you are attempting to bridge this divide by creating meaningful connections for students with the purpose of helping them develop skills in more complex learning. In this third edition text, you explore how to transform your instructional delivery through the process of inquiry. Your goal is to have students achieve higher order thinking by connecting their knowledge and skills into meaningful tasks. Students are encouraged to think more critically and creatively through the process of discovering patterns of understanding and solving problems.

Throughout this book, you will read and work through problems that many teachers encounter today when thinking about the inquiry-oriented learning approach and how to best incorporate it into teaching and professional development.

PLANNING ACTIVITIES TO COMPLEMENT STUDENT MOTIVATION AND INTEREST

Within the inquiry-oriented learning approach, one design goal is to tap into the motivation to learn that your students naturally possess. Students are organically motivated to learn and discover the world around them, especially if it peaks their interest. As you think about your inquiry lesson, find a way to discern this natural intrinsic motivation.

Find out what interests your students early in the school year. Once you gather this information, you will have more specific ideas on how to hook your students in order for them to dig deeper into each lesson. From there, you can carefully plan activities that allow students to solve meaningful problems or work through important issues or concerns using the same tools that experts in the field would use.

Figure 1.2 is an excerpt of a WebQuest that illustrates an active and engaged learning activity that can stimulate and excite students, and ultimately promote new knowledge. This inquiry is best completed in small groups. Each member of the group tackles the quest from the viewpoint of a member of the exploration, such as the captain, pilot, interpreter, secretary, and steward.

Out at Sea WebQuest

You and your team have been assigned as crew members on an up-and-coming exploration into uncharted lands. As part of your role, you will keep the ship's "Journey Journal." At the end of the quest, you and your team will create an infomercial to provide to your benefactors. It is important that you keep good records throughout the journey.

Your team will consist of the following individuals:

- Captain—Sailing the vessel and responsible for the crew
- Pilot—In charge of navigation
- Interpreter—Translates and negotiates with native peoples
- Secretary—Keeps the accounts of the expedition and works with team to make a full account to the King and Queen
- Steward—Responsible for food, water, and comforts, such as heat

Step One: Biographical Information on the Explorer

In order to do a good job for your assigned explorer, you must understand what he or she is trying to achieve, the consequences and benefits of the quest, the time period, and your explorer's personal history. You have heard about many brave explorers who are fearless and travel the world to discover new land, people, and even animals. But what does it take to be an explorer and how might an explorer impact the world as you know it?

To get ready for your adventure, it is important to be familiar with what it means to be an "explorer."

Write down everything you know about explorers in your Journey Journal. *(Teacher Instructions: Wait about a minute and then ask students to share information.)*

Watch a short video to provide a brief introduction. As you watch the video, write down your observations and any questions in your Journey Journal. Explorers always keep good notes and log what they are observing and thinking. *(Stop the video at appropriate intervals to guide student thinking. Ask students to think about what was important or what they noticed in the segment. At the end of the video, ask them to write at least one question that they have about explorers.)*

You should have some good information in your Journey Journal at this point. Let's take another look. What do we know about explorers now? *(Remind students to pull the information they observed from the video into the discussion. Write each of their observations onto the Interactive White Board. Once you have everyone's ideas up on the board, ask students to come up to the board to help organize similar observations. As they move the observations around, ask students what themes they are noticing. Write out the main themes for each group of observations. Once done, make sure to review the themes and have students add each to their Journey Journal. Take a picture and post to your class website for reference. You will access this later in the lesson.)*

Figure 1.2. WebQuest and Inquiry Example

Now that we know just a little more about explorers of the world, it is time to concentrate on your specific explorer. To get started, as a group click on the *Explorer Guide* for your chosen explorer. Once you do, you will be taken to a special page. Your page contains letters and pictures as well as other documents, such as a crew member's journal or even a newspaper clipping. As you analyze each document, answer the corresponding questions. These questions are important because they will focus your thinking to help you analyze each document.

Remember to write what you are finding into your Journey Journal and to work with your fellow team members. Each of you have a specific job duty and each duty is very important in your quest. *(Walk around to each group to make sure they are on task. Ask guiding and open-ended questions as needed about the primary source they are working on. Keep students focused on the question for the assignment and ask them what questions they may have. Point to the themes from the previous activity that were written in their Journey Journal to help them make connections between their research and the themes.)*

Okay everyone, let's get together as a whole class to share your findings. Make sure you have everything ready in your Journey Journal.

Step Two: Team Roles

We have gained a lot of information about what it means to be an explorer and about your specific explorer. Now it is time to prepare for our trip. Remember your roles. You will go to your role to begin your research.

Cargo and Food Report

As you set sail for the exploration, make sure that your ship's cargo list is complete.

Ensure that the ship is fully stocked with food for your crew for the long voyage. Gather information about foods that were available during the time period of your explorer and design a list of items you will need for your ship. Make sure to address such questions as

What will the crew drink?
Will you stop along the way to get more food?
Will you fish or hunt for food?

What else will you bring on your voyage? Investigate additional items your explorer might have brought with him or her by thinking about what kind of clothes were needed, types of tools needed, trading trinkets, or any other items you discover.

When you have your ship's *Cargo and Food Report* completed, add it to your Journey Journal.

Navigator Report

Now that your ship is fully stocked with cargo and food, it is time to set sail. But how will the Captain know where to go? As his or her first mate, it is your job to make sure the Captain has the appropriate maps and directions to reach the intended destination.

(continued)

First, determine how explorers navigated their ships during this time period and report your findings so that the Captain can have those instruments on the ship when it sets sail.

Second, create a map of the journey the explorer took to reach his or her destination. Print out a world map that shows where your explorer began and the route taken to reach the final destination. Make sure you label your map with the following information (*a map website is available for your use*):

- Country that the ship started its voyage in
- Country where the ship ended its voyage
- Body of water the ship traveled across
- Equator and the different hemispheres
- Navigational symbol showing North, South, East, and West

Also, draw a picture of the ship and what it must have looked like when it landed at its destination. Don't forget to take note of such things as wildlife or rivers in your drawing.

Add all these items to your Journey Journal.

Step Three: Achievements of Explorer Report

LAND AHeeeeeaaaad . . .

You have safely made it to your destination!

Now as the first mate, it is your responsibility to act as the reporter to report back to the homeland new discoveries such as

- Where did you land?
- What did you find?
- Were there any native people there?
- Who are they and what are they like?
- Are there raw materials to build homes or survive? What kind of homes might you build?
- Are there plants to eat or should seed be sent over on future voyages?
- What kind of wildlife is there?
- Is this the final destination of the explorer or does he or she set sail soon afterward and explore further

The King and Queen from the explorer's homeland are very curious people, so your report must be detailed and explicit. Your report should be about two pages in length. It should tell of your adventure and the discovery of this new land and what it has to offer. Don't forget to include in your report at least two drawings of your findings so that they can see what this new land looks like.

Add all these items to your Journey Journal.

Figure 1.2. (*continued*)

In this WebQuest, students are provided with questions and primary sources such as letters, images, and agreements that they use in order to discover and explore information. The students then gather primary and secondary information and report on their specific role.

An infomercial highlighting the benefits and consequences of an explorer's quest is the final product. After preparing the infomercial, each team views other peer teams' final products to compare and contrast explorer findings and experiences. This new knowledge is used to compare to other explorers past and present. The infomercials are then published on the Internet to be shared with others outside of the class.

This diverse learning experience provides students with opportunities to learn about and tell the individual stories of each role and then share their findings with group members, the class as a whole, and ultimately extend their knowledge gained to others outside of the classroom.

CASE STUDY

John and Jane Brown are cofounders of the Browns School and from its initial charter they identified a decree:

> Those who enter through the doors of the Browns School will encounter an inviting environment that is filled with a diverse group of learners and dedicated teachers each who demonstrate the desire to learn every day.

From the very beginning, every student that entered the Browns School was engaged to be a lifelong learner around the core curricular areas. But recently with the start of the current academic year, something new was in the air.

It is now the twenty-first century and the community around the school is changing rapidly. Jobs are evolving due to technological advances and globalization. As a result, the local economy in the town is shifting. Some students are not graduating or if they are, they are not going off to college or even working in the local trades.

What can be done to help better prepare students for this twenty-first-century global economy?

A new principal has been hired to spearhead this change. She is an idealistic individual who believes every teacher in the school is ready for a new approach to teaching and learning. Ms. Leeds, the new principal, outlines her challenge with a plan of action. Now, as the new academic year commences, it is time to introduce this plan and get the teachers on board in the Browns School.

The faculty throughout the school have been hearing rumors about change and many are worried. There have been many change initiatives in the past and some have worked for the better and some have not. Many teachers feel frustrated, there is just not enough time in a given day to implement all of these changes. Plus, there is no hard evidence that suggests change is even necessary.

Other teachers are excited. They have heard that an inquiry-oriented learning approach is at the center of the change effort and they cannot wait to learn more about it. How can they incorporate inquiry into their teaching? Many feel that they already incorporate this approach, but they are enthusiastic about exploring new possibilities with teaching and learning in the classroom. Isn't that what inquiry is about anyway?

So, with the mention of change, there is the natural mixture of tension and interest throughout the auditorium as everyone waits for the new principal to take the stage.

Ms. Leeds enters the stage and settles in at the podium. She has a big smile on her face as she welcomes faculty to the new school year. Everyone takes a deep breath and begins to listen to the new plan of action. What they hear turns out to be a challenge to everyone in the room:

"The role of the teacher at the Browns School is to develop each student's passion as a lifelong learner and to take advantage of educational opportunities locally, globally, and virtually. But in this current twenty-first-century environment, we as educators at the Browns School must add one more element.

"We need to help prepare our students to navigate this complex world that we all find ourselves in by helping them develop both critical and creative thinking skills, working with a diverse global community, and being able to collaborate and communicate effectively about each of our content areas in order to better solve the complex problems that they will encounter either in college or in the world of work.

"I am here to say, as your new principal, that it is our responsibility within this community of learners to provide rich experiences for each student to help them better develop the skills needed to be successful in this very complex world. At this moment, I am sure you are asking what this means for each of you sitting in this auditorium.

"Beyond the foundational knowledge that you are teaching your students, you must dig deeper to help create connections and meaning. One way to do this is through the inquiry-oriented approach to learning or what many call a thinking curriculum. We as a community must find ways to work together to make this successful for our students and our school.

"To get started, I have a quest for you. I would like you to divide into your curricular teams and begin finding ways to incorporate inquiry-oriented learning into your curriculum.

"Some questions to consider during your quest:

- How can you incorporate inquiry and authentic experiences into your instruction using technology as a cognitive tool? Discuss how this relates to meaningful learning.
- What does it mean for students to be digital citizens and information literate?
- How can you embed twenty-first-century skills seamlessly throughout your inquiry lesson?
- How can essential questions frame the problem-based learning experience and at the same time scaffold both personal and guided inquiry?
- Are there specific thinking strategies that can be incorporated in your instruction around inquiry?
- How can global connections and telecollaborative learning be integrated into the inquiry learning experience to help students build deeper understanding of the authentic problem?
- What are cognitive tools and how can you incorporate them into your instruction?
- How can blended learning strategies help students interact more directly with the content and one another around an authentic problem?

There is much to learn from answering the above questions and multiple approaches that can be taken. I am interested in finding out how each curricular team interprets the research and makes it their own. I also want to see how you find ways to work across the curriculum. Explore how you are helping your students develop stronger connections with their learning and the world around them.

"Throughout the academic year, you will be presented with challenges to help you design instruction that utilizes the above topic areas. We will come together often, to share and discuss findings and solutions. We are a community of learners and ample opportunity will be provided for reflection and feedback.

"In our teaching community, we will pull together themes and begin building an inquiry framework that can easily be integrated into your instruction to help you design lessons that will be used in your classroom around your standards and learning goals.

"As a teacher at the Browns School, you have been presented with a challenge. Your challenge is to create a framework that you will use to design instruction that incorporates inquiry around authentic problems, twenty-first-century skills, and a more student-centered approach. Review figure 1.1

in your handout to see what elements you should highlight in your inquiry framework. I hope that each of you are as excited as I am! Let's get started."

SUMMARY

This first chapter introduces the idea of inquiry-based teaching and learning. It also underscores why teaching with inquiry is important for educators and students alike in this twenty-first-century global environment. Critical thinking and creative engagement are critical success factors for students today.

Inquiry is the process of engaging in the world around you by asking good questions to discover necessary knowledge and skills. In the classroom, inquiry-based lessons provide students with different ways to view and experience content, work and interact with others, use technology in an authentic way, and cope with and understand complex information.

In addition to content knowledge and skills, awareness of the inquiry process can also be transferred into the real world through further schooling or employment.

Students are naturally curious. One of your lesson design strategies is to harness this curiosity by finding meaningful ways to engage students around your learning goals and their interests. As students learn about course topics, they are encouraged to think more deeply and with greater complexity. They are tasked with gathering and generating information and then doing something meaningful with it.

When looking at your curriculum, identify essential questions that connect your curriculum to the real world. Essential questions are provocative and unanswerable. Their purpose is to stimulate student thinking and entice curiosity. As students begin thinking about an essential question, encourage them to develop their own questions to guide their inquiry and begin connecting their learning to the world in which they live.

At its center, your inquiry lesson should provide a good framework for questions, resources, and student investigation. It should also be wrapped into the context of your learning goals. Think of your framework as scaffolding. It is structured to provide students with assistance at each level of understanding as they move through the inquiry process.

REFLECTION

1. What excites you about your discipline?
2. Define inquiry as it relates to your content area.

3. How can you, at this very moment, relate your subject to the world around you? Pull from local, national, or international news, social media, and so on when answering this question.
4. What essential questions can you pull from your curriculum? What would professionals in the field ask?
5. As you reflect on chapter 1, begin your inquiry framework by including components necessary when planning an inquiry lesson.

Chapter Two

Teaching and Student Learning Using Inquiry

It has been a full day since the faculty meeting with the new principal, Ms. Leeds, at the beginning of the academic year. Throughout the Browns School everyone is beginning to prepare for their respective team meetings.
Each content area team is tasked with the following activities:

- *Review your curriculum map to identify standards that can be enhanced by authentic problem-based inquiry;*
- *Write as many essential questions as you can that highlight the big ideas of your discipline and its relationship to the real world;*
- *Identify possible problems that connect to the big ideas you identified above; and*
- *Identify learning outcomes.*

Ms. Leeds has highlighted that each instructional unit should be centered on what she refers to as a "thinking curriculum": one based on essential questions that tie in authentic problems and use technology as a cognitive tool yielding a more student-centered approach. Your team meeting has been scheduled for this afternoon. How will you prepare?

In this chapter, we explore the multifaceted world of inquiry that involves both critical and creative thinking from an instructional standpoint. You will gain a stronger understanding of incorporating questions to guide your instruction and student learning as you develop a thinking curriculum. Figure 2.1 provides an overview of a thinking curriculum.

This chapter also provides an understanding of the difference between "inquiry" versus "creative" thinking and reinforces how theory impacts the overall teaching practice. It gives insights to designing instruction to include

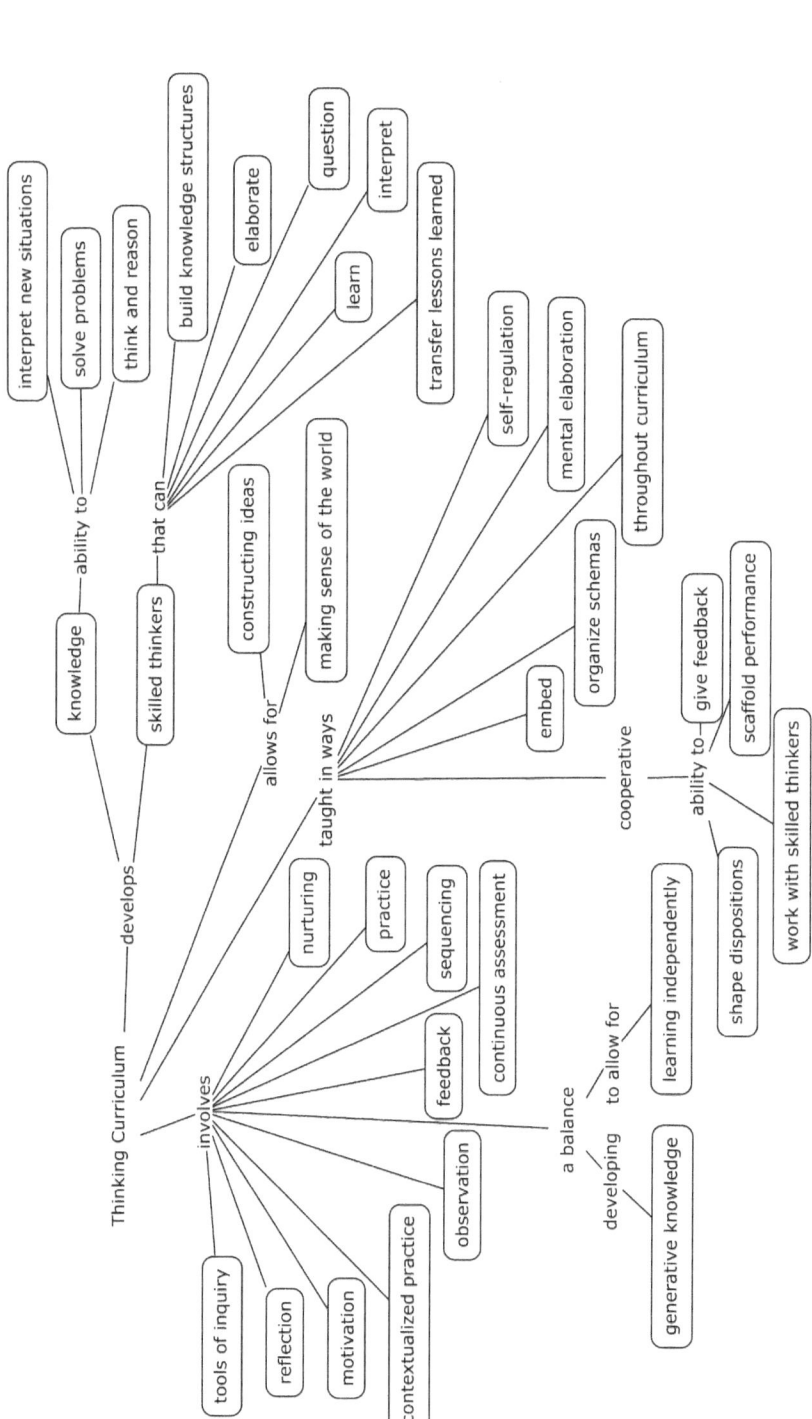

Figure 2.1. Thinking Curriculum Framework

both inquiry and critical thinking. It celebrates innovative thinkers and helps you move your lessons beyond foundational knowledge to knowledge development and construction. It encourages student participation and creation of new and innovative ideas for a larger audience.

USING INQUIRY TO ENHANCE CREATIVITY

Introducing the ideas of a thinking curriculum into both critical and creative thinking can be a difficult task, but it is one that you are ready for. The main premise of a thinking curriculum is inquiry. It allows students to better understand the world by exploring and discovering. One way to do this is to ask good questions and identify quality resources to help analyze, synthesize, and evaluate the "best" answer.

Inquiry ensures that students are not only memorizing required factual information, but are also applying facts to meaningful questions and their own understanding. The questioning approach used throughout the inquiry process allows students to progress from simply holding and finding factual information to being able to apply new knowledge in novel and different ways.

For example, the Yomiuri Land Fun Park near Toyko, Japan, is a maker amusement park where participants can be creative and make things. Visitors take part in developing and building different types of products such as textiles, cars, and food. This entertainment encourages the natural curiosity of visitors, young and old alike.

This hands-on approach to inquiry encourages exploration and discovery of the world by thinking differently, asking questions, and creating or making. Participants are creative and at the same time engaged. How can we transfer this ideology to the classroom?

Inquiry-oriented learning is a creative form of learning where students are encouraged to take an active role in their learning, yet continue to be supported by the teacher. Structure and organization are important elements in any inquiry, along with thoughtful guiding questions and resources to encourage thinking and exploration. As you design your instruction, incorporate each of these elements into your framework. Through inquiry, the focus is on the big picture of the learning unit, why is this important?

Throughout this process

- Identify the educational goals of the lesson along with appropriate objectives.
- Create an authentic and meaningful task. The task must be wrapped around the most important concepts from your activity or lesson that you want students to know.

- Implement continued and authentic assessments that include real-world activities that demonstrate understanding and knowledge creation.
- Facilitate inquiry throughout the learning process to guide students in higher order thinking by having students question and reflect on their findings.
- Be comfortable learning along with your students.

INQUIRY MEANS ASKING QUESTIONS

Inquiry learning focuses on an essential question, a far-reaching even unanswerable question that students attempt to answer while at the same time constructing knowledge and skills about the world around them. Subquestions help guide learning while continuously encouraging students to ask and seek answers to their own questions.

It is important to have students actively involved. You ask questions and students also ask questions by working with their classmates to explore and discover answers. Material is learned through questioning and discovering. Your role is to guide this process to ensure lesson objectives are being met and to allow students to extend and dig deeper. You also need to be aware if students need to take a step back to build or strengthen necessary skills before proceeding.

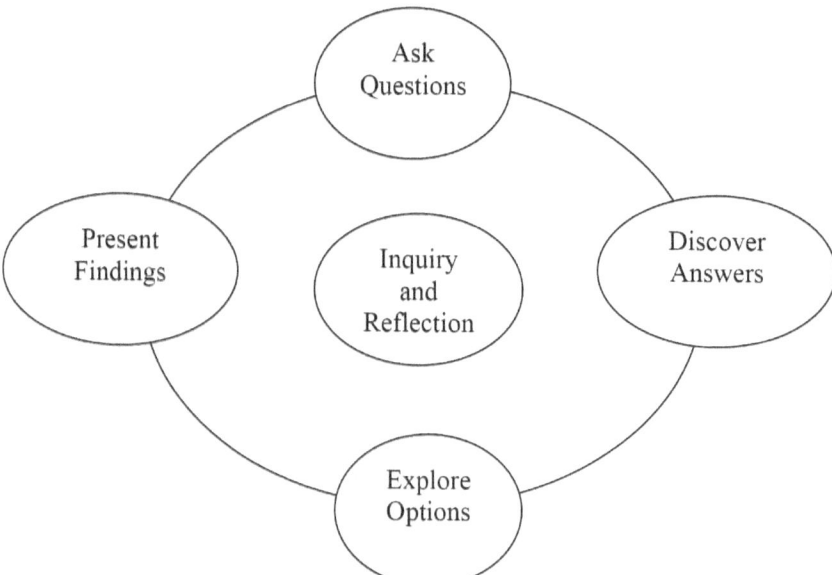

Figure 2.2. Inquiry Process

Inquiry learning is student centered. Students bring their unique knowledge and skills to the learning community. The focus is on the student with an emphasis placed on active engagement in the learning process to develop and build on student understanding. The teacher sets up the activity and facilitates the process to ensure students are on task and learning what is intended.

Inquiry follows a process similar to that shown in figure 2.2. This is a cyclical process and there is continuous movement between each phase. The process begins with questioning and moves through discovery, exploration, and presentation of findings. Throughout this dynamic process questions are introduced, hypotheses are tested, and new questions are formed and reformed.

Central to the inquiry process is reflection and feedback from the teacher and classmates to ensure that understanding and ultimately learning has occurred. A project structure needs to be in place before inquiry-oriented activities commence. Good planning begins with a clearly identified essential question that aligns with the instructional standard and identified learning goals.

PROMOTING AND APPLYING INQUIRY IN YOUR CLASSROOM

To promote inquiry in the classroom, first identify essential questions in your curriculum. The essential questions help pull together your main themes and build connections to real-world events and occurrences. These are broad and overarching questions that guide your instruction, emphasize the main idea of the intended lesson, and are connected to the learning standards. For example, how can I incorporate inquiry throughout my course? Or, what do effective problem solvers look like in my discipline?

Once the essential questions are identified, encourage students to identify subquestions, plan and conduct investigations, and work in small groups to identify solutions or possible answers to the questions posed in your lessons.

As a class, the teacher leads a brainstorming session by posing the essential question. The teacher then guides students to think about themes to identify subquestions. Once the subquestions are identified, as a collective group, the class can decide which questions and categories they want to work on and understand better.

What subquestions, from the questions identified above, would help guide your own learning around incorporating inquiry and a problem-based approach to your teaching? For example:

- How can I encourage student engagement by incorporating active learning techniques?

- What are some effective questions that I could ask before the authentic problem is introduced to get my students hooked and guide their inquiry?
- How will inquiry teaching help my students learn about this standard?

In small groups or as a class, students then begin their inquiry. The notes of the brainstorming session can be saved and posted to the class website so everyone has a reference point to stay connected to the overall goal of the activity. Figure 2.3 outlines the questioning process.

As this example illustrates, throughout the inquiry process students are involved in their own learning. This is true for all inquiry projects. Inquiry learning allows students to develop strategies and methods for deep investigation and exploration into important topics explored in class as they relate to the learner.

Through this process, you are teaching students how to think more critically by asking questions and how to take an active role in their own learning. Inquiry-oriented learning is not passive; rather, it is an active and engaged process that leads to higher order thinking.

Throughout the inquiry process, it is best if students work in collaborative and cooperative groups and as a class to identify what they already know about a given topic as well as what they do not know. Having an opportunity to work through the process of social learning helps students scaffold performances, receive feedback, work with skilled thinkers, and shape dispositions that encourage critical thinking as an important skill that transcends the class.

As the teacher, you encourage students to identify key points of interest about the topic. You also support them as they begin asking deeper questions to explore their interests further as they relate to the intended learning goals for the lesson.

Through this process of collaboration and investigation, students begin to understand the essential question of the lesson and how this fits into the larger picture, such as their personal world. Inquiry is taking shape.

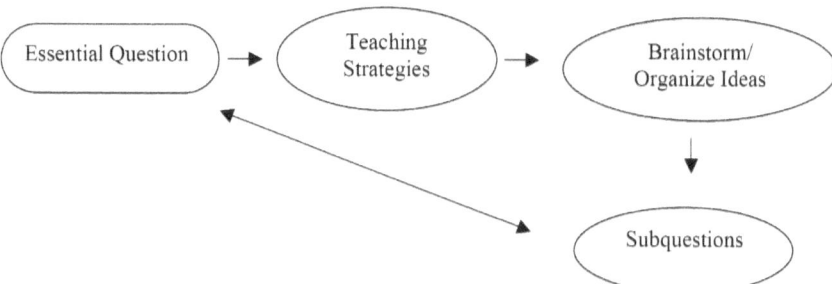

Figure 2.3. Inquiry Questioning Process

A STUDENT-CENTERED APPROACH TO TEACHING AND LEARNING

Although student centered, your students need guidance when working with inquiry activities. As the teacher, you want to ensure all students receive direction in the activity as well as have plenty of opportunities for practice and feedback.

Traditionally, teaching has focused on dispensing knowledge and information to students through lecture, memorization, and skill-specific tasks. After students complete a specific learning objective whether in groups or individually, historically they have completed a paper, a presentation, and/or an assessment. This is not the case with inquiry.

In an inquiry assignment, the teacher provides students with an open-ended question and relevant resources to get them started in their exploration. From there, students are encouraged to ask further questions and are provided resources and tools. Throughout this process, students are developing critical thinking skills to help them tackle the complexity of the task.

Students are often placed into small homogeneous or heterogeneous groups depending on your instructional needs and learning goals so they can conduct research, ask questions, manipulate their data, and ultimately present their findings in meaningful ways such as a debate, an editorial for the local paper, or preparing a letter to a local politician to share information on a political or social topic.

Through this inquiry process, you eventually want students to take the lead in asking questions, investigating good resources, and identifying solutions. However, to fully focus and engage them in the learning process each activity must begin with a good foundation, such as an essential question and quality resources to find the intended information.

The essential question must capture students' attention and encourage them to ask follow-up questions, make predictions, and discover new information. The resources help build on this intrigue and encourage them to explore more deeply. This is called a hook.

A question such as: How well can fiction uncover truth? allows students to creatively explore this concept from a broad perspective and to think critically about fiction literature in general. The answer is not a simple yes or no; instead, they must dig deeper and begin the thinking process.

Ultimately, this essential question allows students to see how this genre impacts life as a whole. Additional layers to this question can be added to the original question as students develop explanations, evaluate predictions, and further expand their understanding. A question is essential when it

- Encourages inquiry around central learning goals and is encompassed around course big ideas.
- Facilitates discussion, critical thinking, motivation and interest, and generates even more questions.
- Allows for consideration of alternatives, justification of ideas and answers, and encourages deeper thought about solutions and evidence.
- Keeps the circle of thinking alive by bringing in prior knowledge and rethinking or retooling of big ideas.
- Enables connections with prior learning and ties in personal experiences and understandings.
- Provides opportunities for transfer of lessons learned to new content areas and ideas.

Now you try it. Formulate an essential question that you want students to investigate and explore, and then relate it back to your course content standards and learning objectives. What is at the center of your subject. What questions come to mind?

Remember, your essential questions encourage students to

- Become self-directed learners intrinsically motivated through their discoveries.
- Work collaboratively with classmates through cooperative learning strategies.
- Become actively engaged in the learning activity and task at hand.
- Share new knowledge through a presentation or performance.
- Develop higher order thinking skills.

GOAL OF INQUIRY-ORIENTED LEARNING

The goal of inquiry-oriented teaching and learning is to design instruction that provides students with purposeful, rich, and dynamic experiences that engage them to think more critically and creatively about content. At the same time, it motivates students by drawing on their natural curiosity and love of learning through exploring instead of merely observing and listening.

Different topics are studied as they relate to various themes. Themes are the organizing principles in which your curriculum is structured and organized. For example, themes could be that of culture, including such enduring understandings of values, beliefs, rituals, communication, or even the ideas of adversity, diversity, conflict, and change. Themes are broad in scope.

Themes also define your curriculum. They provide scaffolding for your hands-on activities, tools, and class resources. As the designer of instruction, you identify themes and build connections for your students around good questions.

These questions develop more complex thinking skills in your students. Crafting questions and then sequencing your questions is important. Your essential question ties your unit together and your subquestions aid in getting your students to a better understanding of your essential question.

As you develop subquestions, consider authentic tasks that are both meaningful and relevant to students, but also support their understanding throughout the inquiry-learning process to ensure that necessary skills and knowledge are learned by the end of the unit.

The overall goal when designing an inquiry project around a meaningful problem is to move beyond foundational knowledge and provide instructional supports throughout, allowing students to deepen their knowledge, expand skills, and enhance their use of technology as a thinking tool.

The end result is that when a successful problem solver is presented with a difficult problem, they sort through their mental toolbox of skills, knowledge sets, cues, and past experiences in order to persist, manage, listen, and think flexibly.

Students continuously learn by questioning and posing better questions. They utilize their past knowledge and experiences to better transfer lessons learned to a new situation. They then gather data to create and innovate and communicate their findings clearly and with passion. This skill sets students up to be lifelong learners.

WHAT DOES TEACHING WITH INQUIRY LOOK LIKE?

You are helping students develop dispositions and skills beyond your curriculum. You are designing lessons that develop these talents by posing difficult and messy questions about the world. Thinking critically and creatively, students then seek resourceful evidence so meaningful decisions can be made. Students are able to reason like a historian, scientist, critic, reader, writer, artist, musician, and so forth.

As you integrate this inquiry approach into your teaching, you open doors to a global audience—in effect, preparing students for the diversity of their global twenty-first-century environment.

Teaching with inquiry involves identifying ways to engage students through authentic investigation that asks them to create and apply models, stories, art work, or even exercise movements. How do you plan for this type of authentic investigation? What do your students need to know and what innovative ways can you use to build structure and design instruction to get them to this point?

Instead of the typical lecture, think about how students can create and share new knowledge with a broader audience as authentically as they gained this new knowledge. For example, by editing or creating a Wikipedia page. By developing an app. By constructing an instructional or informational video posted on YouTube or a website that chronicles history, science, math, art, or health. By creating an augmented reality cartoon, display, model, or even interactive simulations. By conversing and sharing in 140 characters to engage and inform on issues important to them through Twitter.

The inquiry process involves

- Identifying questions to find possible answers.
- Recognizing appropriate and quality resources to aid students in answering the identified questions.
- Manipulating resources to ensure that correct information is identified and answers to specific questions are explored.
- Formulating answers discovered and identifying how these answers relate back to the original questions.

Your role as the teacher in the inquiry process is to create, organize, and then scaffold meaningful activities that engage students and capture their attention. They are then motivated to learn and discover information by asking questions and then share that new knowledge with others in meaningful ways.

SUMMARY

In this chapter, key elements found in a thinking curriculum as it relates to inquiry-oriented activities were identified. The primary goal in inquiry learning is the basis for a thinking curriculum. Pose a question that relates to the learning standards and curricular goals as well as student interests.

Essential questions should be broad and help students think about the bigger picture of the intended learning goals, while subquestions help scaffold learning, resources, and conclusions that take place after the inquiry.

Using an inquiry-oriented learning approach allows students to

- Explore and discover content through an authentic and challenging learning context.
- Create and test a hypothesis through authentic and real-world tools.
- Learn and explore content within a collaborative environment.

- Gain self-efficacy with prior knowledge and expand new knowledge.
- Use technology to enhance and strengthen higher order thinking.

Activities should provide students with opportunities to create hypotheses and then test their hypotheses in small groups or teams. Throughout an activity, students should have ample opportunity to reflect on their understanding and share this new knowledge in authentic contexts. By the end of an activity, students have a product that can be shared with others.

In the chapters that follow, a thinking curriculum is explored in more detail. How to embed new literacies into your course and how you can align pedagogy and learning goals around inquiry are also examined.

REFLECTION

1. As you review the curriculum map for your content area, what are the essential questions that pull the content together? How do these essential questions relate to the community at large?
2. Rewrite each essential question in your own words. The context or focus may change and this is OK.
3. As you examine your essential questions, how do your standards align with them? What is the intended focus of these standards?
4. In reviewing the essential questions of your curriculum for the academic year, what authentic problems or issues can you incorporate to help bring in realistic context? Use news sources, social media, or other resources to gather as many as you can.

Chapter Three

Integrating Computer Technologies as a Cognitive Tool

Ms. Leeds, your principal at the Browns School, is excited about the work you and your team have been doing. She has praised your efforts in reviewing your curriculum and identifying essential questions to present to students. Also, she is thrilled that you have started your research on authentic problems to help students build connections to what they are studying and that you have begun your inquiry design framework.

But what about technology? What are your intentions with regards to technology integration? What resources do you have available and how do you plan to integrate technology tools to help students think more critically about their learning and the content?

You and your team have decided to research using technology as a cognitive tool. Some questions to help with your research include

- *What is a thinking tool?*
- *From your identified standards and goals, how can you integrate digital technologies into your lessons and activities to help students with their thinking process?*

When you incorporate digital technologies with the purpose of actively engaging learners, you enable them to create and reflect on their personal understanding. You provide learning experiences that are designed to activate complex thinking. The learning strategies center on critical thinking rather than just absorbing predetermined information directed by you. At this juncture, you are one step closer to creating a student-centered classroom and using technology as a cognitive tool.

The framework for integrating technology as a cognitive tool in figure 3.1 provides an outline to guide your thinking and activity development.

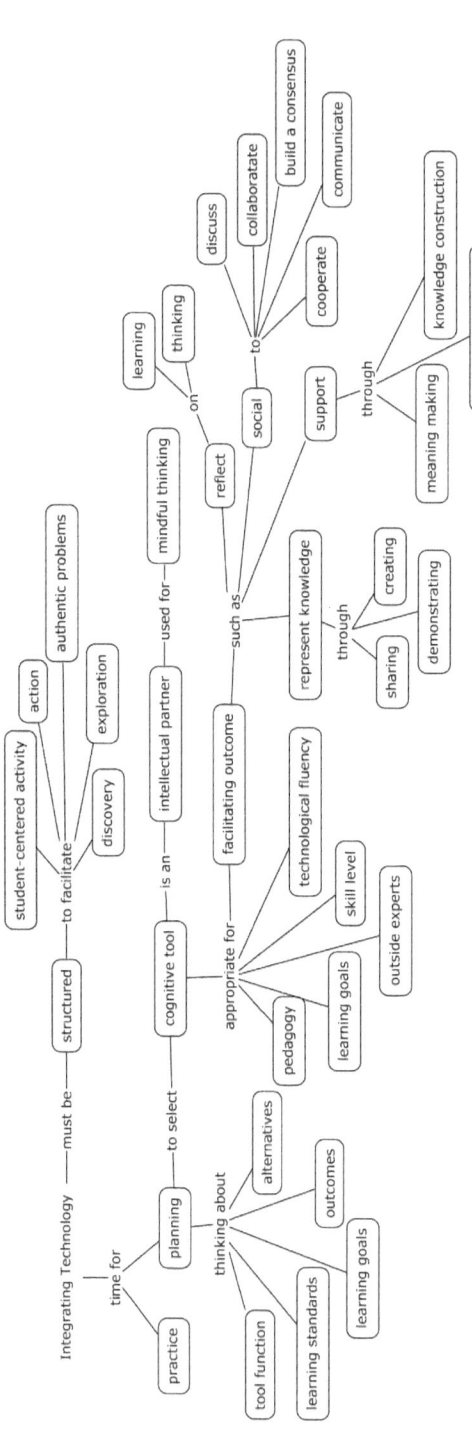

Figure 3.1. Framework for Integrating Technology

For the purposes of this book, technology is defined as digital tools, systems, resources, and devices that are used to generate, store, and/or process and share data. This can include social media, online applications, electronic games, multimedia, productivity applications, cloud computing, and even mobile devices.

Digital learning is defined as learning that is facilitated by instructional practices integrating seamlessly in authentic ways to support communication and collaborative technologies.

DIGITAL TECHNOLOGIES AND THE INQUIRY PROCESS

Digital technologies provide students opportunities to investigate and explore the world just as professionals do in the field. Thus, offering them the ability to think and work like a professional. This applied learning through investigation and exploration using authentic tools around authentic problems is precisely what the inquiry-oriented approach to learning is all about.

Two questions guide your inquiry process as it relates to digital technologies. First, how can digital technologies be integrated seamlessly into your teaching and student learning? And second, how do you know if you are using these technologies authentically?

The power of digital technology tools lies in their ability to provide opportunities for students to communicate, store, retrieve, manipulate, visualize, analyze, and share information with teachers, classmates, and other students and experts outside of the classroom in a global context.

By incorporating technology into your inquiry-based instruction as a cognitive tool, you are able to present opportunities to students to work through the inquiry process in a dynamic way. Within the inquiry design, you are encouraging students to be curious about what they are learning. Through this curiosity, they are empowered to use technology tools in a more authentic manner.

Digital technologies have the ability to systematically organize and focus interest while at the same time stimulate learning through the creation of a realistic environment that combines resources, media, and tools that allow students to experience content in relation to the outside world.

Integrating technology into an inquiry-based lesson challenges you, as the teacher, to think differently about your instruction and your views on student learning: specifically, how integrating technologies can support your teaching and student learning to better create connections around authentic problems and curricular content.

In order to integrate technology in meaningful ways that encourage thinking more like an expert, important decisions must be made about your content, pedagogy, and the technology itself. As well as what to teach and how to teach it. What do your students need to understand? Keep in mind that understanding is defined in a global context as students being flexible learners and thinkers on various topics of study.

As we teach for understanding with technologies, we are identifying tools that will help students think more deeply about content and their own learning. You want to provide those tools that allow students to apply new knowledge, moving beyond a foundational level to one of construction and application, even to generate something new and innovative. This may sound familiar. This is referred to as a "thinking curriculum" and was discussed in chapter 2.

After identifying what students should understand, next recognize how this understanding can be related to an authentic problem. Look at popular news or other media sources to discover these connections—perhaps within your own school. As you do, you will find generative topics that can be aligned with your lesson goals.

As you identify key lesson design elements, think about how digital technologies can be used to help stimulate your students thinking around these generative topics in meaningful ways. For example, download a digital image of an artist's work for an art lesson. Then have students zoom in for a closer look. Pose questions and encourage follow-up questions. Look for answers, and then build connections between the activity and your lesson goals through discussion.

As you consider lesson design and digital technology tools, think about how to seamlessly integrate technology to support and scaffold student learning, all the while allowing students to practice and conduct authentic work using the inquiry process.

USING TECHNOLOGY AS A COGNITIVE TOOL

When you incorporate the inquiry model with digital technologies, you are using technology as a cognitive tool. As you consider how to integrate technology into your instruction using an inquiry model, it is critical to think differently about the technology itself.

The purpose of a cognitive tool is to support deeper and more reflective thinking. Traditionally, technology use in the classroom has been primarily for displaying, reproducing, or recalling information. As you have learned, inquiry-oriented learning does so much more.

It is not a one-size-fits-all approach, but rather it incorporates many different instructional methods and strategies, such as authentic assessments; active participation to connect, collaborate, organize, and create; and engaging your students in realistic contextual learning.

Any technology tool that you incorporate should facilitate exploration and discovery that builds on a student's natural curiosity and develops understanding of course topics. Yet your learning activity must be structured and organized providing good scaffolding for students to be successful. Otherwise, students will not learn what is intended and meaningful learning will not occur.

Technology plays an important role in inquiry learning due to its ability to break down barriers and remove classroom walls. As a cognitive tool, it has the potential to expand opportunities for students to access diverse information and then manipulate and analyze that information in visual or more dynamic ways to create strong connections with the content. See figure 3.2 for an example.

Viewing technology in education as a cognitive tool moves the integration of technology from a device that provides function and features, allowing learning to take place from the device itself, to one of apprentice or

---

Use word clouds, such as the technology tools Wordle or ABCYa.com, to help capture the essence of a body of text and incorporate technology into your lesson or activity as a cognitive tool.

For example, when you type or copy-and-paste content into the text box of your word-cloud-generating tool and click submit, you create a graphic to help students more easily notice what words are important.

You are helping them to sort through or summarize information. Students can use this visual to make comparisons between different texts, improve vocabulary, and even stimulate thinking.

Word clouds have the potential for students to "see" the words to help them identify the context and meaning as it relates to the text.

For example, review the *New York Times* word cloud that highlights every inaugural address throughout American history.

Incorporate inquiry by answering and seeking answers to such questions as

Which presidents used the words "freedom" or "liberty" the most?
What differences were there between parties?

The essence of the message becomes clearer through the word cloud, providing your students an opportunity to see, through a visual image, messages and meanings to stimulate their thinking.

You could add an online analyzer, such as uClassify, to provide an overview of traits, such as personality and mood, providing more data for students to think about and identify even more questions to shape their inquiry.

Figure 3.2.   Technology as a Cognitive Tool: Using Word Clouds

mind-extension that can be used to manipulate and explore information. By thinking about digital technologies differently, for example, as a cognitive tool, you now have the wisdom to understand that technology works best when it supports learning, rather than directs it.

Students' ability to use technologies as a cognitive tool is a twenty-first-century skill. The ability to take diverse sets of information and then manipulate and repurpose it, in order to analyze and think critically to create meaning, is an essential requirement for students today. This is thinking differently.

THE INTERNET AND MOBILE TECHNOLOGIES

The Internet currently serves as one of the most popular and accessible digital tools available in education today. It serves as a complex database that with simple search terms can provide an array of primary sources; blog posts; YouTube videos; local, state, national, and international news; historical information; as well as creation and collaboration applications that can be embedded seamlessly into an inquiry lesson in your classroom.

The Internet is both an information and communications tool. For example, it provides a platform to connect with experts outside of the classroom by videoconferencing, allows access to primary sources—from letters to multimedia—and enables software tools to create.

Mobile technologies are tools such as laptops, tablets, smartphones, MP3 players, and even smart watches and glasses that are portable yet have the ability to connect students to the Internet, multimedia, resources, and people anytime and anywhere.

Steve Jobs, former information technology inventor and entrepreneur, referred to technology as the "bicycle for our minds." In other words, it has the potential, when used as a tool, to take us further than we could have ever imagined.

Mobile technologies have that potential in education when used as a cognitive tool grounded in an authentic context and purpose. Whether you use a mobile device to communicate, create, collect, or interact with data and information, you are providing an opportunity to transfer classroom experiences to real-life situations.

USING TECHNOLOGY IN THE INQUIRY PLANNING PROCESS

In this twenty-first century, digital technology touches many aspects of our everyday world. We communicate via the Internet, receive data from satellites, and record progress through digital images. Technology in the classroom has the potential to provide students with experiences that they will encounter in the world of work or in their everyday lives.

Beyond content knowledge, students are developing a better understanding of media, technology, and information fluency. They are incorporating a variety of technologies that are suitable for the problems they are encountering and thinking about them in the context of the learning goals of the lesson.

During the planning process for your inquiry-oriented lesson, consider the functions of the various technology tools, such as organizing, moving, communicating, creating, copying, and so on, and how they complement your learning goals. Do they fit with your learning goals? Technology can serve as a cognitive tool when it is a partner in the problem-solving process. Its role is not to dominate but rather to complement and extend the learning process.

Also consider the different types of scaffolding strategies, learning styles, technology skills and knowledge, and instructional approaches that can be employed in your lesson. Choose technology tools that meet those specific needs. Technology integration is much more meaningful and effective if you first consider what you need and how the tool can help get you there.

When thinking about what technology to incorporate into your activity, first determine the types of tools you have available and which tools allow students to explore and think most critically and creatively about your content.

As you select technology from an instructional standpoint, consider the following:

- What types of learners are your students? Are they visual, verbal, musical, kinesthetic, interpersonal, intrapersonal, logical, naturalist, and/or existential?
- What are your learning standards seeking? To communicate, collaborate, manipulate, create, debate, discuss, share?
- From past lessons, what did your students *not* understand? Can the interaction between technology tools, content, artifacts, and peers help them develop stronger understanding?

TECHNOLOGY INTEGRATION

Technology integration means more than teaching students how to use a word processor. Integrating technology successfully into a lesson means using the Internet, digital cameras, 3D printers, programming, and software applications as transparent tools.

Technology integration works best when it is student driven. For example, students gather relevant and timely data, aid in analyzing and synthesizing that data, and later present the data in meaningfully ways to the rest of the class. You can even have students think differently and creatively about the new information to solve the problem in a unique way.

In an inquiry-oriented activity, technology tools and the subsequent integration can offer students the ability to

- Access relevant data in a timely manner, such as using primary source documents.
- Collect and record information, such as through an Internet database or spreadsheet.
- Collaborate with experts and other students around the world, such as by asking an expert.
- Present information through multimedia, such as with images, sound, animation, and/or text.
- Have meaningful and authentic assessments, such as real-world problems and projects.
- Present new student knowledge to the world for review and feedback.

SUMMARY

Throughout this chapter, the use of technology as a cognitive tool to engage students in deeper inquiry was explored. Emphasis was placed on how digital technologies provide meaningful, real-world experiences to students as well as opportunities to think more deeply about information instead of just duplicating or recalling it.

Higher order thinking skills of analysis and evaluation were emphasized, while also incorporating creativity by providing opportunities for application and creation of something new. Effective integration of technology and various technology tools were emphasized to assist with practical application.

REFLECTION

1. No technology tool is effective on its own. There are many factors that contribute to a useful tool, such as the context in which it is being used or the interpersonal processes taking place while it is being introduced. How will you scaffold the use of technology as a cognitive tool throughout your inquiry lesson? Provide specific and concrete plans on how you will build

necessary skills, knowledge, and understanding so your lesson goals are successfully achieved in an authentic way.
2. How will your use of digital technologies as a cognitive tool change your pedagogy?
3. As you reflect on chapter 3, what are your key takeaways for consideration when integrating computer technologies as a cognitive tool in your inquiry framework?

SKILL BUILDING ACTIVITY

Create an activity to empower students to interact, design, and produce their own representation of their learning by using technology as a cognitive tool in your inquiry lesson.

Your goal is to

- Review your learning standards to determine which standards would complement using technology as a cognitive tool.
- Identify a hook that will motivate students so they want to explore through inquiry. Your hook should relate to the essential question.
- In your activity, provide opportunities for students to work in teams, as a whole class, and individually to research, manage, and manipulate data.
- Have students share their findings with others. Sharing with a global audience is ideal.
- After they have shared and exchanged findings, allow students to develop something innovative, for example, a new way to solve the problem or think about an issue.
- Have students use technology tools to reflect on their thinking and new representation within the context of their learning.
- Ensure that the technology used is transparent and students are using it in authentic ways.

Chapter Four

Technology Integration Models

You and your team have come a long way since the initial faculty meeting at the start of the academic year. You have learned much more about inquiry-based lessons and have spent considerable time contemplating how technology can be integrated into your classroom and lessons as a cognitive tool. Now it is time for you and your team to begin choosing appropriate technologies that align with your standards and teaching goals.

Before your next team meeting, you and your team will take an inventory of the technologies in your school and then consider which ones can best be integrated into your inquiry lesson to engage students around learning goals and authentic problems. You must begin your preparation soon—as your team meeting is just a few days away.

Review each of the three technology integration models to identify specific classroom practices and technology resources that support your team's curricular goals. In addition, which models are best to support the active engagement of your students in their learning process, helping them obtain information, analyze and synthesize material, and present their learning in meaningful ways around their inquiry?

There are many different applications of technology use in K–12 schools. Some examples include interactive white boards, 3D modeling and printing, Google Maps, smartphones, concept maps and diagrams, as well as social media, object-oriented programming, augmented reality, video, and sound creation tools. The sheer amount and assortment of these technological possibilities can be mind-boggling.

What kind of teaching and learning do these tools encourage? This is an important question that requires consideration as you explore the following three different, yet similar, models of technology integration.

LESSON DESIGN AND TECHNOLOGY INTEGRATION

When considering the integration of technology as a cognitive tool, think about how the tools used will complement your course content and learning goals. Also, consider the skills and knowledge possessed by your students, as well as your own knowledge of both your content and overall pedagogy.

Figure 4.1 provides a visual of how each model and guideline can help focus your instructional design to integrate technology. As with any instructional planning, your methods, instruction, and tools must be balanced, and the needs of students should be monitored at each point during a learning activity. The most important goal is to ensure that each student is progressing and learning what is intended.

A typical course has a number of learning goals as well as learners with diverse abilities, styles, and knowledge so one teaching method, resource, or tool will not be appropriate to match each of these challenges. When reviewing your curriculum, identify where you can incorporate active learning and authentic problems around inquiry using technologies as a seamless thinking tool.

TEACHING METHODS

Generally, there are two types of teaching methods and then several familial parts that tie them together. The first, and the one most applied in classrooms, is the didactic and modeling method. This method is also called direct teaching. You may notice as you walk down the hallway in your school that teachers are standing in front of the room directing instruction, interacting with the resources and technology tools. This is considered an entry level use of technology.

The second model is also used, but often with controls. It is called the indirect or interactive teaching method. This method incorporates opportunities for facilitation, group work, and dialog, and it continues to provide central direction from the teacher with little direction from the students.

The inquiry-oriented approach is more of a student-centered approach. It balances these two approaches, while also helping students develop skills such as leading the dialog, asking good questions, choosing appropriate tools, recognizing quality resources, and seeking appropriate and innovative solutions. As the teacher, you are responsible for planning and organizing this process. You further scaffold their learning and allow for the development of independent yet critical thinkers. Your pedagogy, the art and science of your personal teaching, shapes the method(s) that you incorporate.

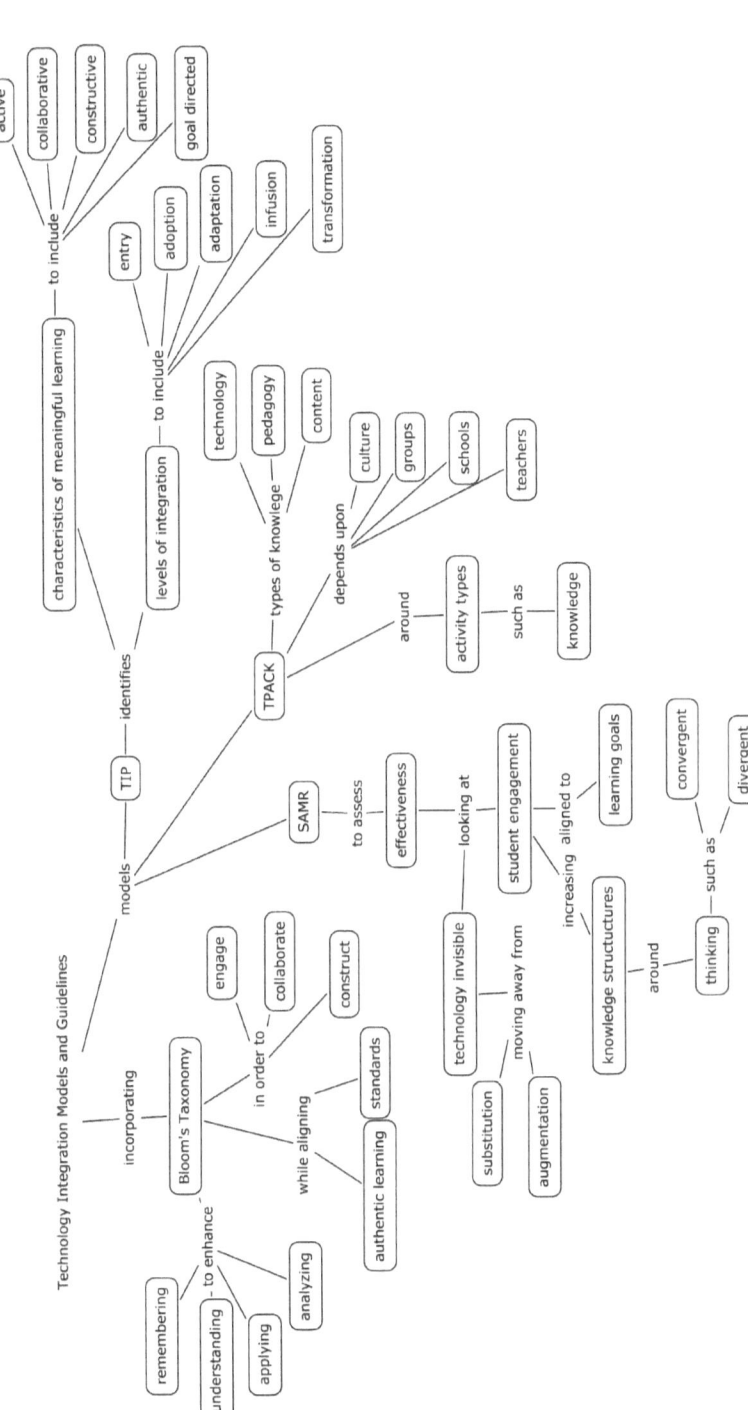

Figure 4.1. Technology Integration Models and Guidelines

In each of the methods above, you identify relationships or familial parts that help you incorporate specific models and teaching strategies. Examples of familial parts include social interactions, processing information, interpersonal and intrapersonal development, skill development, and knowledge construction. Each familial part draws in teaching to bring in a variety of objectives as well as learning goals. Some ways you can break down and even intertwine the above familial parts could be as follows:

- Brainstorm to generate innovative ideas
- Explore a problem or a controversial issue from a variety of viewpoints
- Apply cooperative learning that incorporates diverse groups
- Debate an issue, concern, or idea

As you examine your standards, consider what is the best way to approach each standard. Then, ask if inquiry and higher cognitive processing can be assimilated by tying each standard together more coherently. The goal is to connect your learning goals into more meaningful chunks that provide a better understanding of the goal as well as the authentic nature of the standard itself. This helps to engage your learners by making lessons more meaningful to them.

Next, identify how authentic incorporation of resources and technology tools align with your learning outcomes and determine the overall function and purpose of the technology (discussed in chapter 3) to help students develop a meaningful understanding of your learning goals.

Throughout this chapter, you will review the following technology integration models:

- Technology Integration Matrix (TIM)
- Technology Pedagogy and Content Knowledge (TPACK) framework
- Substitution Augmentation Modification Redefinition (SAMR) model

Each of the above helps to determine how to combine technology as a cognitive tool to match your teaching methods, content knowledge, and learning goals around inquiry.

TECHNOLOGY INTEGRATION MATRIX (TIM)

Developed at the University of South Florida (USF), this technology integration matrix provides a framework to think about the continuum of meaningful learning and for defining and evaluating technology integration. The TIM explores the learning environment—from active to goal-directed, and the level of technology integration—from entry to transformation.

The TIM provides a matrix organizing the different characteristics of meaningful learning, to include

- Active,
- Collaborative,
- Constructive,
- Authentic, and
- Goal-directed learning.

These five areas are then integrated and looped around five levels of technology integration:

- Entry,
- Adoption,
- Adaptation,
- Infusion, and
- Transformation.

Within the TIM there are twenty-five variations of use around each of these characteristics. To take a closer look at this model and the matrix itself, visit the TIM website at the Florida Center for Instructional Technology through USF.

While schools typically remain on the lower end of these characteristics, the goal is to create lessons that require higher levels of cognition and more complex configurations of technology integration. As you critically examine your own pedagogy and lesson goals, think of ways you can incorporate higher levels of technology integration that include adaptation, infusion, and transformation while integrating meaningful learning into each lesson.

Seek opportunities to move beyond students passively interacting with content and technology, such as watching an instructional video and taking notes, or even playing a computer game that introduces them to vocabulary words. Strive for more transformative experiences where students learn necessary skills of monitoring and planning their own learning while using technology seamlessly to explore, manipulate, analyze, and construct information. In so doing, students learn more complex thinking skills and ultimately become self-directed learners.

An example of a more transformative experience could include students creating a trek, perhaps a journey to visit cultural or even historical sites, that has a level of geographic importance using geomapping software. Students gather both basic and complex information from their library and the Internet, finding websites such as government sites, or even primary sources such as letters, images, and video to provide a description, summary, and/or interpretation.

Students can even create their own resources to post from their research. As they are researching, collecting, and thinking about their task, they are working in teams, generating questions, organizing their findings, and beginning the process of authentic work. To learn more about treks, search for Dr. Alice Christie's GoogleTreks. You can use any mapping tool and she provides a valuable resource to begin investigating this type of learning activity.

You can extend this activity to even more tools, such as a spreadsheet and concept map. The spreadsheet provides an opportunity for students to determine patterns from the data and a concept map helps organize research around themes. Throughout the process, students are using technology as a seamless cognitive tool engaging in meaningful work around the learning goal and at the same time moving through the levels of technology integration.

This example provides a transformative and constructive learning experience within the TIM model, where the learning experience provides access to relevant technology tools, online resources, and learning communities. It also provides an opportunity for students to publish their work online to enhance the body of knowledge.

TECHNOLOGY PEDAGOGY AND CONTENT KNOWLEDGE (TPACK) FRAMEWORK

Another model to consider and one that complements the TIM model is the TPACK framework. This framework can be used to design lessons that integrate technology in meaningful ways.

At the heart of the TPACK framework is the complex interplay of three primary forms of knowledge:

- Content Knowledge (CK),
- Pedagogy Knowledge (PK), and
- Technology Knowledge (TK).

The TPACK approach goes beyond seeing these three knowledge bases in isolation. TPACK also emphasizes the new kinds of knowledge that lie at the intersections between them, representing four more knowledge bases applicable to teaching with technology:

- Pedagogical Content Knowledge (PCK),
- Technological Content Knowledge (TCK),
- Technological Pedagogical Knowledge (TPK), and the intersection of all three circles,
- Technological Pedagogical Content Knowledge (TPACK).

The premise of the TPACK approach is to focus on your knowledge regarding content, pedagogy, and technology when designing your lessons. Each of these elements intermingle and are important. You cannot have one without the other, hence the emphasis on "technological pedagogical content knowledge."

This framework examines the uniqueness of your discipline, specifically what skills and knowledge students need to gain mastery of, and the skills and knowledge they currently possess about your content, as well as technology use. It also recognizes that each of these components varies between age groups, teachers, schools, and culture; and understands that each situation is distinctive.

This combination of content, pedagogy, and technology knowledge means more than simply adding technology to a traditional teaching and learning model. The goal of the TPACK approach is to determine how technologies can best be used to access and process content knowledge and then understand how technologies can be used to support and enhance student learning.

The TPACK model encourages you to think about how to incorporate creative connections between what your students are learning (content), how it is being taught (pedagogy), and appropriate tools (technology).

With this framework, it is important to consider the technologies that you incorporate and how they are most appropriate for your learning environment, such as interactions that you want to develop and sustain between students and you as the teacher, and as a support to learning.

Also, consider students' prior knowledge and experiences with the content, technology, and even culture, as well as how the activities match the routines and norms of your classroom, and finally whether the tools and resources match the learning activity to support your learning goals.

When planning instruction, identify your learning goals, build teaching strategies and methods around appropriate activities that organize and direct the learning experience, and provide appropriate tools and resources to engage learners and achieve the intended learning goals.

To help with this, the TPACK model identifies activity types that you can combine to provide an active and engaging learning experience that aligns to multiple standards. They include *knowledge construction*, as well as *convergent and divergent* thinking.

Just like in the TIM model, it is important for students to gain foundational knowledge through such strategies as effective questioning, comprehending a text, or conducting an Internet search while developing capacities to construct more complex understanding.

You can incorporate knowledge construction, as well as convergent and divergent types of activities into a single lesson providing opportunities for students to develop or strengthen their foundational understanding and build even deeper knowledge.

Beyond being able to construct knowledge by answering a direct question on a worksheet, students can "converge" on the same conclusions from a variety of approaches such as creating a chart or timeline, or "diverge" from a conclusion in order to think differently or creatively by building a model, creating a game, or even an app.

In an art class studying the visual arts, technology is integrated to align with the learning experiences. The focus is not on simply using technology but rather the effective and seamless integration.

Example 1: View a static piece of art.

Students connect with the art through augmented reality or by accessing a digital archive, such as the Google Art Project.

Example 2: Research and explore art-related methods, techniques, viewpoints, and history.

Students analyze, interview, and then synthesize findings and results.

When conducting research online, students use a social bookmarking tool to take notes, organize, and share their findings. They use Skype to interview a curator at the local museum. They also create timelines to showcase a linear development of this art form.

Example 3: Use what has been learned about a specific art form and apply this new knowledge to create a unique piece of art by pulling in the ideas and research studied.

Utilize a variety of mediums—such as animation, photography, or Web 2.0 tools—to share this new art form with others.

Figure 4.2. Examples of Knowledge Construction with Convergent and Divergent Thinking

Within each lesson, this combination of activities and the variety incorporated into a lesson creates flexible learning structures. These structures provide a multitude of learning opportunities, and with appropriate planning, allow students to build deeper connections to the content in meaningful and realistic ways. See figure 4.2 for an illustration.

This combination of activities demonstrates that each activity is a component of a whole. The example incorporates a variety of learning goals, while using appropriate technology tools, coupled with a teaching style that engages students in exploring and then applying what they learned.

Knowledge construction, as well as convergent and divergent thinking, each help contribute to the cognitive processing that represents how students are formulating what is important from the content and then applying appropriate technologies in the process.

SUBSTITUTION AUGMENTATION MODIFICATION REDEFINITION (SAMR) MODEL

After applying best practices in using technology when designing lessons to the above two models, it is now time to begin thinking about effectiveness. The SAMR model is useful for that purpose.

The SAMR model looks at how you progress through technology integration. Specifically, how you use technology to increase student engagement with the learning goal and the continuum where technology becomes a more meaningful and well-used tool in your classroom, one that is invisible but central to your instructional practice.

Levels of computer technology within the SAMR model include

- Substitution
- Augmentation
- Modification
- Redefinition

Within the SAMR approach, the goal is for integration of technology to transform learning experiences by both redefining and modifying learning tasks to achieve curricular goals. See figure 4.3 for an example.

As the example illustrates, in order to apply the SAMR approach effectively, you must create meaningful opportunities for students to develop and build, and then redesign their knowledge structures through the process of divergent or creative thinking.

> You are teaching about a great novel, such as *The Great Gatsby* by F. Scott Fitzgerald, in an English class. The traditional assignment would be to have students read the paperback version of the novel.
>
> Instead, below is how this assignment would work using the SAMR approach:
>
> - Substitution: Students read the online version of the novel.
> - Augmentation: Students use an online thesaurus, dictionary, study guides, maps, and a historical website to supplement and add to the reading.
> - Modification: Multimedia resources such as text, images, video, and audio are utilized to complement the knowledge and understanding of a character in the novel. Students construct the character, bringing him or her to life.
> - Redefinition: An essential question is asked that incorporates culture and change as themes.
>
> As a class, students identify subquestions and key elements by using a concept mapping tool.
>
> Students create multimedia to add to the message they will present by posting to the class weblog. The course blog will be accessed by a professor and her students at the local college, who will critique student understanding and engage students in dialog about their findings.

Figure 4.3. SAMR Model Example

TWENTY-FIRST-CENTURY SKILLS AND MEANINGFUL LEARNING

As you consider your inquiry-oriented activity and how best to integrate technology tools, it is important to include twenty-first-century skills, such as communication, managing projects, and using technology, as well as the National Educational Technology Standards for Students (NETs) developed by the International Society for Technology in Education (ISTE).

By incorporating inquiry-oriented learning into your lessons, you move beyond basic subject or content mastery to more sophisticated thinking about real-world skills and ideas as they relate to your curricular area. As discussed earlier, inquiry-oriented activities allow students to use higher order thinking skills such as analysis, evaluating, and creating.

NETs provides standards of integrating technology tools into teaching and learning to enhance student skills. These include

- Creativity and innovation (developing innovative products and processes)
- Communication and collaboration (using technology tools to support learning)

- Research and information fluency (utilizing technology tools to gather, evaluate, and apply information)
- Critical thinking, problem solving, and decision making (analyzing and synthesizing new knowledge)
- Digital citizenship (understanding ethical uses of technology and equity issues)
- Technology operations and concepts (knowledge of the language, systems, and operations of technology tools)

Bloom's Taxonomy	Technology Integration Activities
Remembering: memory retrieves information	• Highlight a phrase or word on a social bookmarking site. • Copy information into an online note program. • Locate and bookmark a resource.
Understanding: constructing meaning from different ideas	• Tweet a new discovery in own words. • Tag a blog post. • Annotate a webpage. • Comment on a blog reflection adding to the discussion. • Blog reflection journal on a focused reflection task.
Applying: what is learned is used	• Upload content to share with others in the cloud. • Retrieve appropriate data from an online database, calculate and create a chart using a spreadsheet, and then edit to display to a group.
Analyzing: breaking down ideas into parts and then determining which parts interrelate	• Research, evaluate, add, remove, and alter content on a *Wikipedia* page in order to add to the body of knowledge. • Deconstruct a reading to create a concept map to organize content around themes. • Add hyperlinks to a blog post to organize and add more in-depth information.
Evaluating: making judgments based on specific criteria	• Identify a hypothesis about a cause to a problem. • Develop a personal learning network (PLN) around specific interests and instructional goals. • Make judgments from research, test theories, reflect on new information and prior experiences, and then post in a public forum for debate.
Creating: putting diverse ideas together to form a whole	• Adapt a digital product using a variety of tools and build on a body of evidence to showcase a new interpretation of an idea, concept, or problem. • Build a website around a curricular goal as an educational tool for others to access, comment on, and contribute to.

Figure 4.4. Bloom's Taxonomy and Technology Integration Activities

When adjusting your lessons to an inquiry approach integrating technology to promote meaningful learning, move away from using technology solely to deliver or augment content. Instead, identify standards that provide opportunities for students to become actively involved with the content, while at the same time encouraging them to think more critically.

Figure 4.4 provides an outline for moving along Bloom's Taxonomy with appropriate technology integration activities. Bloom's provides a framework for categorizing educational goals and using technology integration as a tool.

When thinking about Bloom's Taxonomy, remember that when you select a digital technology it depends on the type of learning you want students to engage in and the activity's level of difficulty. Bloom's Taxonomy can help match technology tool functions with your learning objectives through action words.

As you design your inquiry-oriented activity, identify how you want students to demonstrate their understanding of the major concepts and themes they are exploring. Ask yourself the following questions:

- Can technology provide a medium for students to express themselves and share their new knowledge with others in a meaningful way?
- What will students be able to do or know once they finish this inquiry activity and how can they share it with others?
- How can real-world examples or artifacts be incorporated into the inquiry-oriented activity to engage students and get them to think and explore the bigger picture?
- How can technology enhance learning opportunities, such as incorporating ideas or discussions of experts in the field by using a resource such as ePals, Skype, Twitter, or a weblog?

SUMMARY

In this chapter you were introduced to three technology integration models to help guide your thinking around your content, pedagogy, and available technology to design inquiry-based lessons that allow students to explore and think about what they are learning while they are learning. Each of these models has a website that you can access online to see specific examples of how to integrate their frameworks into your own teaching to help guide your instruction and student learning.

As you think about integrating technology as a cognitive tool, consider each of these three models, your own learning goals and teaching pedagogy, as well as your students' needs. Then strive to incorporate varied ways for students to use digital tools authentically to help create a meaningful learning experience and environment.

REFLECTION

1. Of the three technology integration models introduced in this chapter, which resonates with you most in terms of your own teaching strategies and overall pedagogy?
2. What are three takeaways from each model (TIM, TPACK, and SAMR)?
3. Review the NETs standards from ISTE on integrating technology tools into your teaching and student learning. How can you incorporate these six areas (creativity and innovation, digital citizenship, and so on) into your inquiry project?
4. Define the twenty-first-century learner. Describe the twenty-first-century teacher. How do both relate to meaningful learning and Bloom's Taxonomy?
5. As you reflect on chapter 4, add each of the technology integration models and the NETs standards into your inquiry framework.

SKILL BUILDING ACTIVITY

Practice using the ideas and concepts presented from the various models in this chapter. Strive to integrate technology as a transformative learning tool in your inquiry lesson to ensure students become active learners and engage in critical and creative thinking around your curricular topic.

The information introduced in this chapter stresses the importance of technology as a cognitive tool, but it is you, the teacher, who must design meaningful learning experiences that use good teaching strategies and methods, coupled with appropriate technology tools and resources centered on your intended learning goals.

Go back to the activity that you completed in chapter 3 and identify where you can enhance the activity using the information you learned from each of the technology integration models discussed in chapter 4. How can you move students from being passive observers of information to active learners, that is, students who are able to manipulate content and think about a complex topic in novel ways using technology as a cognitive tool?

Be explicit in describing which aspects of the various technology integration models you incorporated and why. Provide examples as appropriate. Examine how incorporating these three models into your inquiry project relates to meaningful learning and twenty-first-century skills.

Chapter Five

Social Media and Collaboration

You and your team are developing a solid framework for your inquiry lesson. This includes identifying learning goals and standards. It likewise includes an authentic problem to wrap your inquiry around. Learning about technology integration is critical also—both from the standpoint of viewing technology as a cognitive tool and utilizing the various models to help provide a framework when designing your lessons to include technology.

Now the principal, Ms. Leeds, wants you to integrate social media tools and strategies to incorporate more opportunities for students to collaborate, connect, and communicate.

As part of the initial planning process for this new task, you and your team have identified a guiding question focused on social media and collaboration to direct your research and design before the next staff meeting. Given the knowledge you have gained thus far with your team about inquiry-oriented teaching and learning around an authentic problem, the question is as follows:

> *How can social media provide a medium for students to interact more meaningfully with one another, you as the teacher, and those outside of the classroom, as well as to reflect on their learning and gain timely feedback while enhancing the inquiry lesson?*

You decide to develop a plan of action to present at the next faculty meeting along with an example to give other faculty a starting point in considering this important question.

The use of social media within education provides many possibilities to unite students and educators with a touch of a button, click of a mouse, and an

Internet connection to collaborate, communicate, create, and share. Life has been transformed for most everyone around the globe.

Whether you keep in touch with other professionals or personal friendships through social media tools such as Twitter, LinkedIn, or Skype, or use share and collaboration tools such as Coggle, Diigo, or Google Docs, information and community can easily be available at any time of the day or night.

Teaching and learning in this social context can be just as seamless, transforming the way students interact and share with others by creating opportunities to learn in a more authentic and meaningful way. This chapter explores integrating social and collaborative learning experiences into your lessons to help students build stronger connections with one another, their own learning, and those outside of the classroom through the integration of social media. See figure 5.1.

SOCIAL MEDIA AND TECHNOLOGY

Social media aligns well with both the connectivist and social constructivist models of learning. Within each of these models, learning occurs best when it is active and the learner's curiosity is able to provoke the experience in a social context.

When you consider integrating technology as a social and cognitive tool, think of digital devices connected to the Internet that facilitate social interaction. These devices make collaboration and sharing of ideas and information possible.

Technology tools include blogs and wikis; media such as audio, images, video, and text; and sharing platforms such as Facebook, Ning, and virtual worlds. These tools allow students to message as well as create content that can be manipulated, repurposed, and shared immediately. From an instructional perspective, these tools have the potential to create, distribute, and interact with content in a social context and can make the learning experience more authentic.

Consider ways to align instructional technology tools with learning goals in your class to provide opportunities for students to collaborate, create, and manipulate their own stories and then distribute them to a larger audience for discourse, debate, and even remake. In your planning, ensure that you scaffold the learning process around good instructional design and regulated learning. As the teacher, you also want to provide a solid foundation in digital literacy, such as identity, safety, and presence in an online culture.

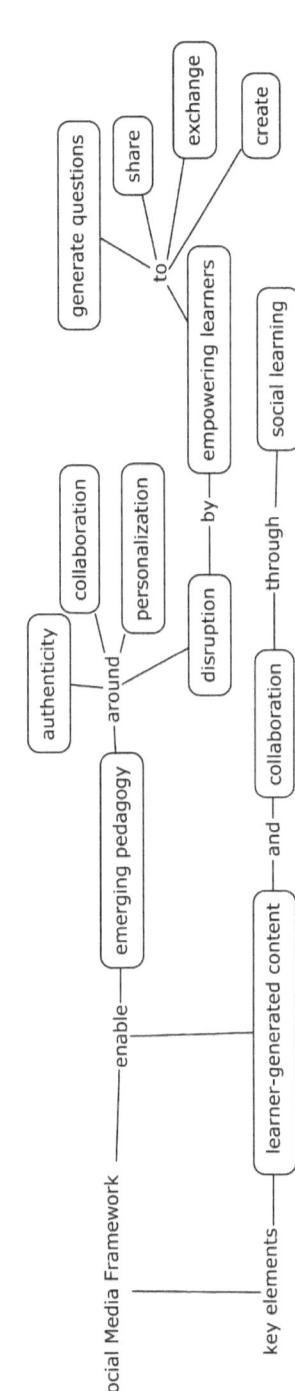

Figure 5.1 Social Media Framework

DESIGNING INSTRUCTION USING SOCIAL MEDIA

Throughout this book, you have been actively seeking ways to construct learning experiences that encourage students to interact with content and one another in a more authentic and meaningful context around your learning goals through essential questions. Social media is a digital technology that is designed to align with these goals.

As an educator, you are aware that students develop strong social connections through collaboration and interactions with others. Through dialogue, presentation, exchanging, and exploring diverse beliefs, and questioning existing conceptual frameworks, students engage in your curricular content.

How can the use of social media be integrated into your inquiry lesson to promote these ideals of collaboration and connection? What do you want students to understand during the lesson and at its conclusion? As you examine your outcomes and learning goals, notice that alignment around constructing and challenging knowledge within a social context is a perfect match for social media integration.

A sampling of performances that apply, for example, could be having students translate, interpret, apply, and/or form complex ideas into new patterns, make judgments, perform, and create. Social media enhances these outcomes by providing an interactive and social progression.

Social media is a form of Web 2.0 or the "read-write-Web." It allows users to "socialize" with others via the Internet through the process of

- Sharing resources and content—using tools such as Twitter, Pinterest, Diigo, and Evernote
- Collaboration—using tools such as Google Docs, Timeline.js, Tribe, Twiddla, Popplet, or Google Maps
- Exchanging information—through discussions, debate, likes, and comments using tools such as Yammer, Wikispaces, Facebook, CoveritLive, or Google Hangouts
- Opening your class up to a wider range of resources, sources, and experts—using digital databases such as search engines, raw data sites, libraries, and websites such as Ask an Expert
- Allowing students to write and learn from a professional audience—using tools such as blogs and wikis

Web 2.0 provides opportunities for you and your students to develop self-regulated skills, engage in collaborative learning, solve complex and authentic problems, and develop relationships around a personal learning community. At the same time, students are able to access, create, aggregate, modify, and distribute knowledge all while having the potential to make meaningful connections to and with others easily and flexibly using the Internet.

There are some disadvantages of using social media in your classroom, but with good planning and preparation these problems can be lessened. First, students can become distracted by the ease and amount of information that is available and may begin to socialize or go off on a personal or different tangent.

For your part, ensure that the tools that are being introduced are for educational purposes and that students remain focused and on task. Having a continuous model of feedback to ensure questions are answered as they occur is a terrific way to assist with this.

Another disadvantage could be students accessing inappropriate content on the Web. Ensure that social media policies are in place to reduce this issue, while still encouraging participation in social interactions and use. Teaching digital citizenship and digital literacy skills would help (see chapters 6 and 7). A system such as Google Classroom or tools such as Edmodo or Saywire to monitor interactions can also be used.

COLLABORATION AND A SENSE OF COMMUNITY

Collaboration is as dynamic as our global and interconnected world. We have developed into a global economy that is connected through telecommunications, allowing virtual teams around the world to contribute to projects. In order to be a global citizen, it is important to be self-directed and work individually as well as in teams to effectively collaborate with colleagues at a distance.

There are many benefits for integrating social media into your classroom. Along with self-directed learning, these include powerful opportunities for

- Collaborative learning,
- Internationalization,
- Networking,
- Improving interpersonal skills,
- Practicing digital literacy, and
- Personal knowledge construction.

In effect, you are teaching students necessary global citizenship skills along with content knowledge in a supportive educational environment.

A social media integration activity is highlighted in figure 5.2. It explores interacting with information in a collaborative way while also using social media seamlessly as a cognitive tool to empower students to think and work

Students are tasked with writing an interactive poem using social media. There will be one unified voice, yet group members will contribute their individual research and singular voice using social media tools.

Collaborative poems can be written on any topic across the curriculum. The goal is for students to demonstrate knowledge of imagery around a time period, event, or even a mathematical equation by incorporating research and lessons learned in the activity.

Restate the essential question for the activity and the inquiry that has been completed to date.

Open up Coggle, a mind-mapping tool, to brainstorm what everyone learned in the lesson. Lead the class to identify different themes and compare them with the themes identified at the beginning of the lesson. Ask students what themes are most relatable and then divide them into teams around those themes.

Team members are instructed to work with their diverse groups and share responsibilities, practice online safety, demonstrate ethical use of the Internet, and communicate respectfully and clearly.

The class backchannel, "Today's Meet," is the online chat for posting questions and sharing information with the class for this lesson. Each student is responsible for checking this backchannel and participating in the backchannel by either answering questions or sharing information.

In teams, students must decide as a group what to write about in the interactive poem.

A team leader is assigned who accesses the class Diigo site, a social bookmarking website, and identifies where each team member will add bookmarks and annotations. The team leader is responsible for keeping everyone in the group on task.

A Twitter hashtag is also identified for the group to tweet about their findings.

During this point in the activity, you walk around and guide students with questions or remind them about how to evaluate a resource.

When the group research is completed, the team recorder opens up Evernote, a note-taking tool, in order to take group notes.

The team leader from one group pulls up the Twitter hashtag and each team member shares and presents their research. Some found experts in the field and explored their blog posts and Twitter feeds. One of the team members asked one of the experts, a person who works in the industry, a question and they tweeted back! The discussion was productive and it was decided that they had a good start.

Now it is time to start the team Google Doc so that each team member's theme can be added to the document. Links to the Diigo site, the class Coggle mind map, and the Evernote page are added to the document as a reference.

Figure 5.2. Social Media Integration Example

> It is getting close to the end of class, so team members lay out their expectations for working on the project.
>
> Each team member agrees to work on their portion of the poem outside of class and write in the Google Doc under their assigned theme. They will discuss and share their work in class tomorrow.
>
> From there, they can begin composing their poem as a group.
>
> In class the following day, students share what they had written the night before and make a few edits. In one group, a couple of the team members decide they want to create their own media to emphasize their theme. One creates a comic and the other creates a 30-second video.
>
> The team decides to use Twine, a tool for telling interactive nonlinear stories.
>
> Each student wants to type in their portion of the poem. It's about two paragraphs each. As a group, they decide to add hyperlinks to at least one resource per theme to add more information about the concept or topic in order to provide additional emphasis.
>
> The two students who made their own media finish and add their content to the interactive poem.
>
> As a team they read and discuss the flow of the poem. Does it identify the key ideas of what they learned in the lesson? Is it in one voice? Does the media added provide emphasis to achieve their goal?
>
> They make a few changes and then as a group write a paragraph introducing their interactive poem. They post it, including the link to the Twine page, to the class weblog. Now they are ready to share with the class!

meaningfully and to take ownership of their knowledge creation. This activity provides an opportunity for learners to work as a collaborative group using technology in an authentic way to connect, create, and then share information with others.

An overview of how specific social media tools can provide connections is shown below:

- Coggle: A social mind-mapping tool to identify themes and connections.
- Today's Meet: A backchannel to share information and ask questions.
- Social bookmarking: A tool such as Diigo is used to annotate, categorize, store, and share resources.
- Microblogs: A platform such as Twitter around a class and group hashtag to share research, information, and resources; and to connect with a larger audience outside of the classroom.

- Evernote: To organize and take notes that are shared with the group.
- Google Docs: To provide a space for each group member to write their portion of the activity and receive feedback and suggestions.
- One-minute videos: Using a tool such as Animoto to highlight the message.
- Toondoo: To create a cartoon to convey a difficult point.
- Twine: An interactive nonlinear story tool to present the activity with hyperlinks to relevant resources, video, and the cartoon.

A good place to learn more about social media and networks is the Classroom 2.0 community. This is a supportive community of educators who are learning more about social media and how these tools can be integrated into teaching.

In designing your inquiry lesson, identify ways to support instruction to engage students in innovative thinking and problem solving by using social media tools. Many students are already using and participating in some form of social media and are thus searching or producing content. This is an inquiry process.

Social media provides an opportunity to reach outside of the classroom to engage with experts as well as produce and share with a wider audience. Social media has the potential to strengthen the following skills when used with inquiry:

- Cognitive or physical, such as multitasking and logical thinking
- Social, such as persistence, peer-to-peer learning, risk taking, and general knowledge
- Technical, such as technical confidence, designing and creation, and hand-eye coordination

By integrating social media into your inquiry lesson, you are supporting instruction around student needs and interests. At the same time, you have the potential for students to connect and collaborate with others outside of the classroom, such as experts or even other students and teachers around the world (see chapter 9), all while helping students develop necessary digital skills.

SUMMARY

This chapter explores the use of social media and incorporating social media tools into your teaching and student learning to improve and increase collaboration and communication. Social media tools can support and build community by providing richer experiences for relationships with experts and students from other classes in different parts of the world.

Social media allows students to plan, create, curate, produce, and share their work. Just like any digital tool, social media is a way to provide an authentic experience for students built around your learning goals.

Social media needs to be balanced between other types of communication and knowledge-sharing opportunities. And there are certainly disadvantages, such as information overload, distractions, privacy issues, and online safety concerns. When designing instruction, carefully plan for rules of use just like with any other technology tool integrated into your teaching.

REFLECTION

1. Planning is an important component to be used when implementing social media into your inquiry-oriented lesson. You want to encourage interaction between students, as well as the creation and dissemination of new understanding. Part of the planning process requires having specific learning goals and outcomes that align with the functions of social media. It is also important to ensure that students are familiar with the rules and procedures for using social media safely and ethically as outlined by the class and school policy. Given all of the above issues in managing the planning process, how will you plan for and approach the use of social media tools within your instruction?
2. Which specific social media tools do you believe will most complement your instruction?
3. What type of social media would you incorporate into your inquiry-based lesson and authentic problem?
4. How could you incorporate collaboration into your inquiry framework?

SKILL BUILDING ACTIVITY

One of the most powerful uses of technology in schools today is its application to socialization, allowing users to collaborate and share with others seamlessly.

The saying that "two heads are better than one" is particularly true when you incorporate social media into your lessons. Learning socially means you want students to work with one another, experts in the field, and even teachers in other classes to explore and learn about complex topics using telecommunication technologies.

Create an activity with the purpose of using social media to engage students to work collaboratively on your authentic problem in the inquiry lesson. Your activity should use at least one social media technology tool (preferably more) and have students actively involved with others to work through a problem, scenario, or idea, and then share it with a global audience for discourse and debate.

Chapter Six

Digital Citizenship

You are now about halfway through the academic term and concerns over students' ethical, legal, and appropriate technology use are being questioned by your principal, Ms. Leeds. How can you convince her that your students ARE solid digital citizens capable of living and interacting with information and data online safely and appropriately?

Ms. Leeds asks your team to answer the following questions before the next faculty meeting:

- *How can you design instruction that uses technology as a cognitive tool, but also reflects the important aspects of being a digital citizen?*
- *Consider how your students currently practice safety and privacy online. Are they knowledgeable about cyberbullying? Do they understand their digital footprint?*
- *How will you allow for equitable use of digital technologies to all students in your class?*

You had better get started. Ms. Leeds expects evidence for the next faculty meeting.

Digital citizenship encompasses being able to connect, create, and collaborate safely, securely, and ethically. It also includes the need to consider equal access for all as well as ensuring digital skills in navigating, online privacy, virtual safety, and cyberbullying. This chapter reviews digital citizenship in terms of appropriate and responsible behavior as it relates to using technology in your instruction and student learning. It explores modeling appropriate behavior and teaching your students these necessary skills.

WHAT IS DIGITAL CITIZENSHIP ANYWAY?

Just like citizenship in our nonvirtual lives, offline, and away from mobile devices, when we interact on the Internet we are participating as a citizen, but in digital form. How digital information and content is managed and our moral and ethical interactions with it play a role in digital citizenship.

Within your instruction, digital citizenship embodies practices that facilitate the knowledge and skills necessary for students to think critically, as well as conduct themselves ethically, appropriately, and responsibly in this diverse and dynamic digital landscape. Figure 6.1 provides a framework to consider as you design lessons to incorporate digital citizenship.

Incorporating digital citizenship seamlessly throughout a lesson involves being familiar with the following:

- Being safe online and when on digital devices
- How to best interact, use, and even repurpose information found or left online
- How to remain private when online
- Who you should give credit to and why
- Appropriate ways to collaborate and communicate with others online

Students begin building and developing digital social skills, as well as cultural competencies, early in their lives. Many are even developing digital identities at this very moment, but they do not necessarily know how to be effective digital citizens. As their teacher, you can help them with this.

To provide these necessary skills to your students and make sure that each student has equal access to a variety of technologies, even if and especially if, they do not have such access outside of your classroom is an important component of teaching the twenty-first-century learner. It is important that this be done both efficiently and safely, especially in light of the ever growing online participatory social culture that social media presents to students every day (discussed in chapter 5).

Thus, along with digital literacy or technology fluency and information literacies (discussed in chapter 7), there is also a need for your lessons to include skills and knowledge necessary to be a solid digital citizen.

DIGITAL CULTURE

We live in a digital culture where educators are no longer the sole provider of knowledge. Students now easily and quickly peruse the Internet for information.

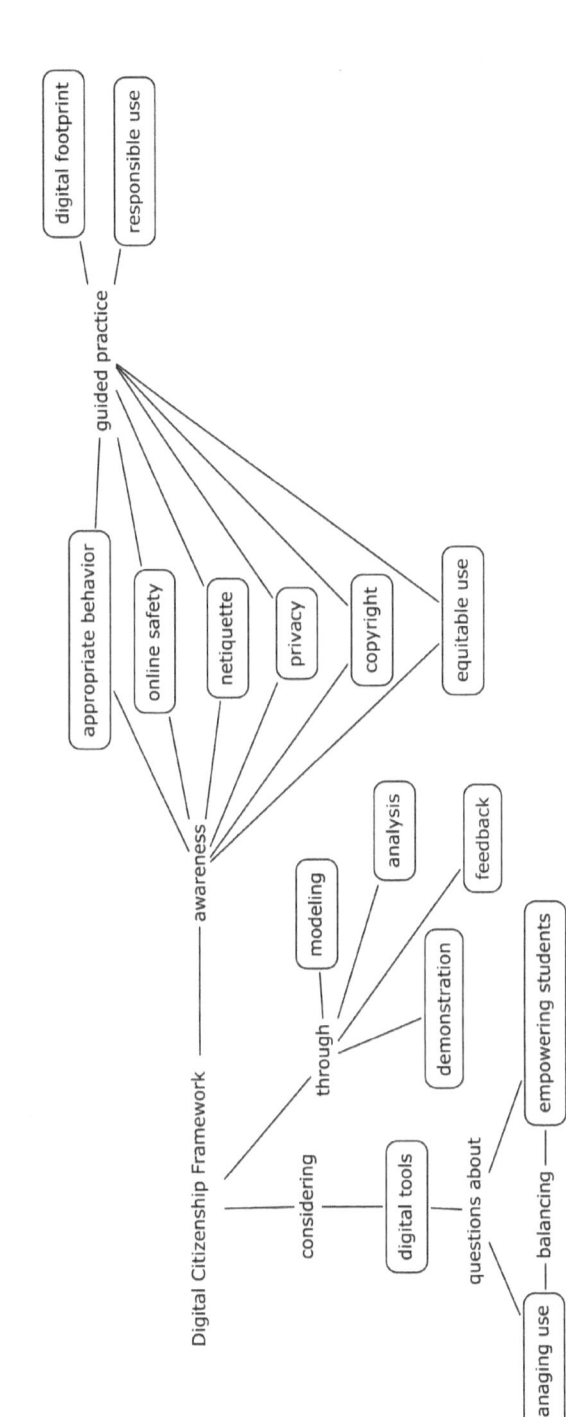

Figure 6.1. Digital Citizenship Framework

In this digital world, connected learning means a new responsibility for teachers to provide students with meaningful and authentic learning experiences to enhance and improve their digital literacy as well as deepen content knowledge.

As a citizen in today's knowledge-based global world, we all must effectively and critically navigate, evaluate, and create information using a range of digital technologies as well as be cognizant of safety and the ethical and legal ramifications of using and sharing this information.

Digital literacy builds upon the traditional forms of literacy in that its focus is on ensuring responsible digital citizens. This is true in any media platform—whether blogging on a social network site, solving a math problem within an online course management system, or reading and editing a post in a wiki.

Think differently. Your students may have limitless technology and information at their fingertips, but

- Can they access that information efficiently and effectively?
- Can they evaluate it critically and competently, and identify objective facts from propaganda?
- Do they understand the ethical, legal, and moral issues concerning access to and use of information?
- Can they create meaning from data?
- Do they have appropriate access?
- Do they practice safety online?

In essence, are students aware of the value of information and the rules and procedures of participating online, aside from what is needed to pass a test, write a research paper, or complete a PowerPoint presentation?

Today's students are digital natives or Net Geners. Between the ages of eleven and thirty, they have grown up in a hyperlinked and interconnected world. Digital natives prefer

- Freedom of choice
- Customization
- Transparency
- Entertainment and play
- Collaboration
- Quick communication
- Opportunities to be innovative or creative

Granted, not all students have access to technology at home or outside of school, but the number who do seems to be growing dramatically. And the digital natives of today need guidance in this highly connected world on being a productive and conscientious digital citizen.

Anyone older than age thirty is considered a digital immigrant and grew up before the technology boom. As an educator, where do you fall on this continuum and what do you need to prepare yourself and your teaching?

With this chasm between digital natives and digital immigrants comes a big responsibility for teachers to model best practices around digital citizenship. We must utilize technologies and find appropriate Internet resources seamlessly so that we are preparing digital citizens for the twenty-first century and beyond.

COPYRIGHT AND CREATIVE COMMONS

Protecting intellectual property is taken very seriously in the United States. Copyright holders defend their rights quite vigorously, and as a teacher you should think carefully about how you and your students use the works of others in terms of music, video, spoken, and written words.

Copyright protects the rights of any creator of content, even your students. It gives the creator of content, even content posted online, legal control to do with their works as they choose. Once you create an original work, you then have exclusive rights to sell, make copies, make other works based upon it, or place it on public display. The types of original content protected by copyright laws include literary, dramatic, musical, artistic, and certain intellectual works.

As mentioned above, copyright protection also extends to you and your students. The assignments you create for class or the notes students take in class and post online can be copyright protected. At the same time, you may see something online or in print that you want to use in your class. Is this possible? Or are you restricted under copyright protection?

This may all sound a bit daunting; however, there are some limitations to these rights and exceptions. In general, teachers apply what is called "fair use" to much of the content used in their classrooms. This exception allows for copying of *some* copyrighted material for a limited and transformative purpose, such as to comment upon, criticize, or parody a copyrighted work during in-class instruction. Such uses can be done without permission from the copyright owner for a limited amount of time.

In other words, fair use is a defense against a claim of copyright infringement. If your use qualifies as fair use, then it would not be considered a prohibited infringement.

An alternative to restrictions of copyright is called a Creative Commons license. This license permits a content creator to give explicit permission to those wishing to use their intellectual property or original work in a way that respect the owner's wishes and thus eliminates the need to contact the content creator. The idea is to continue the philosophy of a free and open Internet, one that allows information to be equitable and more accessible throughout the digital community.

As part of your lesson, provide opportunities for students to share their work and allow for others to use and remix their work by setting up a Creative Commons copyright license. Use the Creative Commons website to create a license for the original work you create in class.

With all the restrictiveness of copyright, you are probably wondering what sorts of content you can put into your online or blended course (discussed in chapter 11). There is a remedy called the TEACH Act of 2002. The Technology, Education and Copyright Harmonization (TEACH) Act identifies that you do not have the same rights in distance education with copyrighted information as you do in a face-to-face traditional lecture class, so it attempts to clarify what use is permitted in an online or blended course.

Even though there are some boundaries and limitations, there is more room for you to display copyrighted work within the online component of a course if certain conditions are met, such as proper citations, a notice to students that the work is subject to copyright protection, and a notification that materials cannot be transferred to anyone not enrolled in the course. Review the TEACH Act as well as fair use and copyright requirements before posting copyrighted information online.

INCORPORATING DIGITAL CITIZENSHIP INTO YOUR INQUIRY UNIT

As you design lessons in your class, you should always incorporate digital citizenship ideals. You are modeling behavior that helps students engage positively in actively practicing good citizenship. It also gives them an opportunity to reflect on why digital citizenship is important and what that requires every time they interact with information and digital technologies.

It is important that these skills not be thought of as isolated. Instead, they are similar to the skills of a traditional literacy curriculum. You are helping students become knowledgeable on how to use and create information safely and appropriately online, as well as how to be smart consumers and users of the Internet and other digital technologies.

You are also training them to be cognizant of the power of the Internet, for example, nothing is deleted and nothing is truly private. As an active user, you are always aware of your digital footprint—that is, the message you are telling about yourself online—and how to be safe.

As you develop lessons and activities, build in the norms of appropriate and responsible behavior when using technology. Students should understand that this digital access is an authentic community of users, but not everyone has the same access or opportunities. With access they have opportunities to explore, connect, create, and collaborate with others virtually with an Internet connection.

Structure your lessons and build a classroom culture that is supportive, one that is safe and demands responsible use. Incorporating inquiry can provide a framework to help develop these skills and knowledge. Encourage students to ask questions about digital use and think critically about interactions.

A valuable resource can be found at the Common Sense Media website. Common Sense Media is a free treasure trove of resources for educators and parents. Once you register, you have access to scope and sequence documents, as well as curriculum containing lessons and videos for grades K–5, 6–8, and 9–12.

Each time you or your students post on a public website, class reflection blog, personal reflection blog, wiki page, or a site such as VoiceThread to create and then share new knowledge and skills in an online environment, it is public information. As a result, it is imperative students behave responsibly by giving creative credit and adhere to copyright requirements. They can practice safety by thinking critically about what they choose to post and share about themselves online.

An understanding of responsibility in this digital landscape is essential. Students have a responsibility to themselves, their classmates, family, and the larger digital community. When students post in this authentic medium, they must be cognizant of their responsibility as digital citizens. With every post or interaction online, they are leaving a trail or footprint.

Teach students about being aware of their digital footprint, both their passive footprint (a trail of searches and interactions on websites that are collecting data without their knowledge) and their active footprint (a trail that is created when they interact with information online, from a simple tweet to an Instagram page).

SUMMARY

Digital citizenship is an essential skill in this digital landscape. It helps us navigate the concerns of cyberbullying, privacy, safety, and equitable use. It informs us of our interactions online, or our digital footprint. As you integrate technology into your curriculum, you are teaching students norms of appropriate use and responsible behavior, as well as how to actively participate in this digital society.

It is important for you, as the teacher, to model these behaviors and skills of being a digital citizen. You are also designing authentic experiences that allow students to interact, create, and share by actively participating in the creation of a digital footprint and reflecting on their own technology use as well as that of others.

REFLECTION

1. Consider what it means to be a citizen in today's world. One part of our citizenship involves interactions within a digital landscape. Within this landscape, the moment we access the Internet or pick up our smartphone, we practice specific and definite responsibilities and behaviors. From confirming that your students are accessing appropriate websites and are on task, to ensuring that they remain safe and ethical, how will you manage, model, demonstrate, discuss, and provide opportunities for students to use technologies appropriately and securely?
2. How will you ensure that all students have equal access to a variety of technologies and learn these important skills when designing and implementing your lessons?
3. Where in your inquiry framework can you incorporate the necessary skills required of a responsible digital citizen so your students can practice and receive feedback to develop these skills?

SKILL BUILDING ACTIVITY

Throughout this chapter, you explored digital citizenship with the ultimate goal to identify specific ways that you can incorporate these necessary skills and knowledge into your lessons. There are two main questions from this chapter:

- How can you most effectively embed these ideas into your curriculum in order to challenge students to think critically about safety, privacy, security, relationships and communication, cyberbullying, their digital footprint and reputation, along with self-image and identity?
- How can you ensure equitable and ethical appropriate use in students' daily usage of the Internet and other digital technologies?

Incorporate your thoughts holistically on the above questions into your inquiry lesson.

Select one topic from the list below to explore and present to students:

- Internet Safety
- Privacy and Security
- Relationships and Communication
- Cyberbullying
- Digital Footprint and Reputation
- Self-image and Identity
- Creative Credit and Copyright

Design and create an interactive presentation to engage students around your curricular goal and inquiry problem based on your selected topic from above. Gear your activity toward a certain demographic, such as age, grade level, curricular problem, and so on, so that it authentically allows students to learn, reflect, receive feedback, and practice the necessary skills involved in your topic selection.

Chapter Seven
Information Literacy

You and your team realize that learning about new technologies is a gradual process and as a result, you are making incremental changes in your pedagogy to incorporate a thinking curriculum. You also recognize that digital fluency skills, such as information literacy, need to be embedded into each lesson.

Students appear to be having some difficulties in the lessons with incorporating problem-solving strategies. They are not always sure what type of information is needed and then have a hard time discerning how to effectively and efficiently locate, evaluate, and use this information to support their new understanding appropriately. In addition, students seem a bit bewildered with all the diverse information available to them on the Internet.

You and your team decide to ensure that students learn the competencies to identify, develop, and practice specific information literacy and problem-solving skills to be more successful with their academic work as well as general use of the Internet. But there is a lot to consider. You decide to do some research before you convene for your next meeting. What type of research would be most meaningful?

As you design for inquiry, you are incorporating new literacies, digital and informational, throughout activities due to the authentic nature of both.

Digital and information literacies involve students performing as skilled users who are able to effectively find appropriate information and then critically think about the material discovered, paying attention to its message so they can effectively organize, synthesize, and analyze. As discussed in chapter 6, using the new knowledge through quoting, or adapting it through paraphrasing and summarizing, builds upon student skills of ethical and legal use.

These "soft" skills are critical success factors in the twenty-first-century environment and can be seamlessly integrated throughout your inquiry lesson. This chapter explores digital and information literacies and provides approaches you can take to incorporate them into your inquiry activities.

INQUIRY AND THE OPEN CLASSROOM

Through inquiry learning, students become actively involved in the inquiry activity by incorporating information literacy skills when solving problems. Skills such as observing, collecting, analyzing, and synthesizing information are developed in order to make predictions and draw conclusions. Inquiry-oriented learning allows students to discover and pursue information with active and engaged involvement in the material.

In today's world, the classroom is no longer closed. Instead, it is open and available through the Internet. Each time you access and use information found on the Internet or in digital databases in the library, you are teaching and modeling to students that knowledge is shared and accessible.

Within activities and lessons, strive to provide learning experiences that develop, teach, and encourage students to think critically about information found online. Promote inquiry and critical thinking to help students consider how best to access, evaluate, use, create, and ultimately communicate information.

Embedding knowledge and skills across the curriculum can support students in becoming independent lifelong learners using inquiry and critical thinking skills. They are able to recognize the need for information, formulate questions based on information needs, identify potential sources, and then develop and use successful strategies for locating information. All while incorporating technology as a learning and thinking tool.

Students also need to evaluate information critically and competently by determining accuracy, relevancy, and comprehensiveness. It is important that they be able to distinguish fact from opinion, recognize inaccurate or misleading information, select content that is relevant to the identified problem, gather data and information from multiple perspectives and contexts, and then derive meaning from the information presented in a variety of formats.

Using available technologies to find and organize information in order to best apply it, integrating content into current understanding, building on a current knowledge base, and respecting property rights are also necessary skills for students to hone.

As the teacher, you can scaffold the learning progression and use the inquiry process to help students build and practice these necessary skills by completing meaningful activities that showcase the importance of developing these digital and information literacy skills, allow for practice and feedback, and illustrate how this knowledge extends beyond the classroom walls.

INFORMATION LITERACY

Information literacy involves thinking skills that are derived from the traditional literacies of reading, research, and writing. It is a problem-solving approach that requires inquiry—asking questions and seeking answers—by finding relevant and appropriate information, forming opinions, and evaluating a variety of resources to ensure that informed decisions are made. Figure 7.1 provides an overview of this approach.

Within your curriculum, you want students to learn how to locate information and then how to translate, describe, and summarize it. As they do this, students apply their information literacy skills to include even more complex topics and searches. Analysis occurs through the process of breaking down information into its component parts and students are able to build on the knowledge gained.

Evaluation occurs when students are able to make informed judgments about the information and new knowledge is gained and used to determine if it is appropriate in helping solve a problem. If so, students organize all component parts of the new information in order to create something new, thereby generating a new idea or performance.

These critical information literacy skills can be taught at all levels, even in the early years of a child's education. The level of challenge, appropriate pace, and depth and breadth of scope are different depending on the individual development, but digital and information literacies can and should be present in every classroom at every grade level.

The rationale behind these required skills is that students should be able to find information, evaluate different data sources, and exercise good judgment. They should also be keen on how to appropriately use information as well as critically evaluate if the material should be used.

Being information literate also means that students develop skills necessary to pool knowledge with others to help solve complex challenges, negotiate between diverse communities, and follow threads of information and material that may include video, images, written work, and online resources.

Today's twenty-first-century digital and information literate global learner should be able to

- Recognize the need to locate reputable information to solve problems and generate ideas;

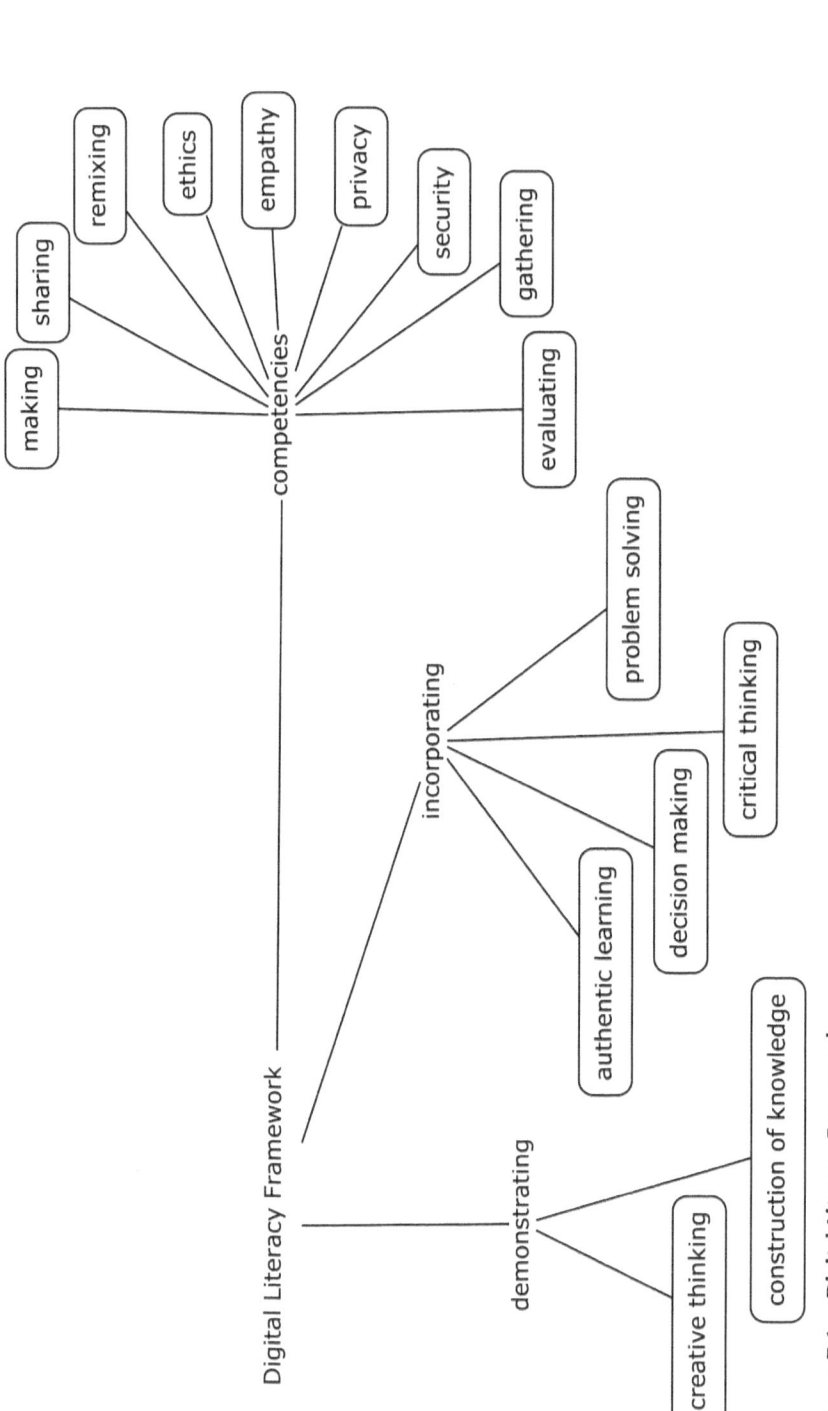

Figure 7.1. Digital Literacy Framework

- Formulate higher order questions that identify specific information needs pertinent to their inquiry quest or problem;
- Integrate prior knowledge with new information to build understanding around complex topics and ideas;
- Locate diverse information with varying views and reference sources;
- Develop strategies to identify effective and applicable search terms to narrow search results for better accuracy of information received;
- Create organized systems around data and information with appropriate themes identified; and
- Critically and resourcefully use new information to solve complex problems that may or may not have clearly defined solutions.

Throughout this inquiry process, varying types of information, such as video, personal blog postings, news websites, and images are examined. The information must be interpreted from the source and it is the student's responsibility to perform the critical thinking required.

Digging deeply into a topic makes students more informed citizens. Deep analysis forces students to think about search terms, decipher information from varying viewpoints and resources, and then think and ultimately apply new information in dynamic ways.

Information literacy ensures that students explore issues, ideas, and opinions in more detail and from a variety of sources and viewpoints in order to make an informed decision. To do this, students must have the skills to gather all types of information from visual, text, sound, personal opinion, and so forth in order to better synthesize and analyze.

This embodies a lifelong or twenty-first-century learner: someone who is self-directed, who explores and investigates information; a person who looks at various and different points of view and is able to change opinions and ideas when they are well informed. This individual moves beyond the surface with inquiry investigation and poses important questions from a variety of sources.

EVALUATING WEB RESOURCES

One important skill in information literacy is evaluating Internet sources. Whether you are a skilled evaluator of online resources or not, it is likely that you will benefit from knowing how to search and research the Internet more efficiently and effectively.

In *Teaching Zack to Think,* Alan November recounts a story about a student who was asked by his teacher to write a paper on the Holocaust. Using his own knowledge and skills of information literacy, the student found what he thought was a knowledgeable reference source and began writing his report. However, the resource this student located turned out not to be such a reputable source. It was biased and untrue.

How can you prepare students to think critically about information found online?

How can they be better prepared in using the Internet as a technology tool?

It is important to be able to critically evaluate Web resources for authenticity, applicability, authorship, bias, and usability. A good evaluation tool is a must, both for you and your research, and you will need an age appropriate tool for students to use during their work online.

Use an evaluation criterion when integrating any information found online into a lesson or activity, modeling to students necessary critical thinking skills when acquiring information and then using it for meaningful learning.

INCORPORATING DIGITAL AND INFORMATION LITERACIES INTO YOUR INQUIRY UNIT

As you incorporate digital and information literacies into your inquiry unit and across the curriculum, consider these skills as foundational elements that students need to know to be successful learners and critical thinkers. Just as with digital citizenship skills, it is important that these skills not be thought of in isolation. Instead, work to embed these throughout your course to help students develop and build information literacy skills so they are informed and knowledgeable users of information and digital technologies.

Once you and your students have located quality resources, they can then be organized and stored using a curation tool such as Pinterest, Diigo, or Delicious. They can also be tagged or given a short word that helps categorize the resource and makes it easier to retrieve. Using a social bookmarking tool and a cloud-based service allows you to easily share what you found with others. This ultimately allows for the creation of a community of individuals who hold the same interests, thereby building a social connection to the content and information.

After you have developed your own quality resources for a lesson activity, you can teach your students about credible sources and some effective strategies to find good sources (see figure 7.2). This example provides an approach to help introduce effective Internet search strategies to students. This can be expanded and included within other digital literacy lessons. This helps

In a lesson on the Civil War, students will learn about issues that divided the nation, including specific events and battles, leaders that emerged, the daily life of citizens, as well as the aftermath of the war itself.

Each of these topics includes several subtopics. Each topic and subtopic has its own information and resources.

You help students develop a research strategy and provide scaffolding around the thinking required to begin researching and searching on the Internet in order for students to be as efficient as possible.

You begin by asking students to think of search keywords, synonyms, or key phrases related to the Civil War. You request that students be as specific as possible to help identify the main topic or idea so that when one term or phrase is mentioned, it helps to identify and even define the topic. This is similar to a connect-the-dots game, as you begin connecting the dots, you are able to identify the picture contained within.

When beginning a search, you instruct students to create a list of keywords that describe the topic and try to limit these keywords to no more than five. This helps to keep the search more manageable, especially in the beginning. As students search and conduct their research, they begin identifying new terms that help refine their query.

You also introduce students to the use of quotation marks to find the exact words in the exact order, such as "US Civil War." Next, you show them how a minus sign in the search criteria has the ability to limit a word from your search such as Washington –Redskins, and how to limit searches to specific groups or organizations. You also offer that if students use a string, by incorporating each of these strategies into their search, they can narrow their search even more.

You develop a game for students to play so they can practice. Those with the fewest hits in 10 minutes win the game. You have students work in pairs to practice new search strategies and you pose a question to answer that will help introduce the Civil War in your activity. Students use their new skills to answer the question. As part of the game, they must organize their search using a chart to record search terms, strategy, and the results received.

Once a team wins, have them project their search string on the interactive white board and explain their strategy to the class. You can do this several times with new questions to have students practice and receive feedback. For future lessons, add more strategies and terms helping students to build new digital and information literacy skills.

Test your questions used for this activity before handing off to students, as the Internet is a dynamic, ever-changing tool, and websites and information can easily change, be replaced or deleted. As students play the game, walk around the room to monitor group progress and answer questions.

Figure 7.2. Digital and Information Literacies Activity

students understand the importance of using successful strategies to secure relevant information and find reputable information online.

As you teach students about the importance of critically evaluating Web resources, you also want to identify an evaluation tool. Review a wide variety of resources available online, such as Kathy Schrock's Critical Evaluation Surveys and the ABC's of Web Site Evaluation. These tools provide assistance with determining quality and reputable Internet resources to help you and your students create a tool that works for your content area and age group.

Modeling and demonstrating good practice is important in any lesson. But it is especially important when you ask students to find good information and use information appropriately.

Throughout your lesson, provide mini-activities around key topics. To continue with the example in figure 7.2, illustrate the different views of the North and South, abolitionists, leaders, and/or specific artifacts (such as letters from family members) that students can explore to discover a factual understanding of the Civil War. Encourage questions when students investigate these resources by providing open-ended questions. Ask them to predict what may happen given different scenarios.

The main premise is to teach students to think more critically about resources when generating ideas and to carefully choose good resources to better determine a solution. During the lesson, identify key words and have students create an index to organize and define these words. Students can use these key words for their own research to develop a digital story. The entire lesson, all the way up to the digital story, is a building block.

After your lesson, engage students in critical thinking by navigating and collecting information from primary source websites that include, for example, policies led by government officials or images of certain events. Students will see that primary resources can provide an unfiltered view, which may be very different from that written in popular literature. During this entire process, through the lessons researched and resources gathered, students learn about the Civil War in a meaningful way.

Once each of these mini-activities are completed, students can work in small groups to further explore a person or issue to create a digital story. Possibly they could even create a Twitter account for the family members, local leaders, and politicians themselves. What would they say? Now students must think directly about digital technologies and how these individuals would use these resources for their cause.

Students practice these literacy skills and then defend their choices by being proficient with the research generated. They could present their dialog in Twitter on the class website and support their findings as to why their characters shared what they did in this medium and how what they shared may have changed the course of history.

In the above examples, students are learning while doing. They are utilizing technologies that they are familiar with, but at the same time they are adding to their skill set by learning specific strategies and skills around information literacy and digital citizenship.

And, in this example, students are extending their thinking to predict how leaders and citizens during the Civil War may have used these same digital tools for their causes. This type of activity requires students to be flexible, take initiative, and produce something creative. At the same time, they are responsible digital citizens that are information literate.

SUMMARY

Information literacy is an important skill set for students and for you as the teacher to gain when working with the Internet and its vast resources. It is a strategic process that requires organization as well as specific strategies in order to successfully find, evaluate, and use information in various formats to create new information for personal, social, and/or global purposes.

In order for students to develop these digital and information literacies, it is important to provide opportunities to develop the critical thinking skills required to be successful through direct experience that includes practice using authentic problems and quality resources.

REFLECTION

1. How will you design lessons that allow students to think critically about information in your curriculum? Provide an overview.
2. What specific information literacy strategies can you use to have students make sense of information gathered from diverse sources so they can practice identifying misconceptions and supporting main ideas? How can you encourage them to think critically about recognizing and assimilating conflicting information, varied point of views, and bias?
3. How will you use social bookmarking or a curation tool to store, organize, and distribute resources to students and then have students contribute to this resource?
4. As you reflect on chapter 7, identify key areas related to information literacy to incorporate into your inquiry framework.

SKILL BUILDING ACTIVITY

Throughout this chapter, you explored how to create a lesson that incorporates information literacy. The focus was on engaging students to think critically about the variety of resources they use to solve complex problems.

Now it is your turn to create an activity that frames a specific query around a learning goal. Provide students with an opportunity to experience what credible information is when solving a problem. Incorporate specific thinking strategies to use when searching for good information.

In developing your activity, have students

- Identify good questions to help guide their search for quality information.
- Identify specific information that they need to solve their problem—asking questions such as: What do I need to know? What kind of information should I gather? What information do I already know? What gaps in knowledge do I have?
- From this initial questioning, identify search terms, synonyms, and phrases they can use to find specific information.
- Use an evaluation tool to identify appropriate sources.
- Organize information found in meaningful and logical ways.
- Use information from a variety of sources and viewpoints; then assess this information found with other viewpoints and sources.
- Take notes to help understand the information through comments and reflection.
- Share findings effectively, complying with copyright laws and intellectual property.

Chapter Eight

Engaging in Problem-Based Learning

You and your team have been researching and planning your authentic problem around your identified curriculum goals, but you realize that you need to have a good plan in place to help you achieve these goals while still meeting the curriculum requirements.

In your plan

- *Ensure that the problem identified aligns with your learning goals and is meaningful to students;*
- *Identify the interdisciplinary nature of your problem;*
- *Facilitate problem solving and scaffold inquiry skills; and*
- *Determine appropriate technology tools that support collaboration and engage students in thinking.*

You and your team decide that since this is your first true problem-based lesson you will start small so it is not daunting to you, the teachers, or your students. As a team, you do a simple search online to identify some possible problems for investigation. You decide on one that aligns with your learning goals.

You agree to meet again tomorrow to identify an essential question, resources, technology tools, and scaffolding activities that will help students both become effective problem solvers and at the same time make connections to your intended learning goals. This will be a busy week. Everyone is excited to get started.

Problem-based learning is designed around a real-world problem, challenge, or scenario using an open-ended question tied to your curriculum. In this student-centered approach, your students learn about your learning objectives through experiences as they investigate a "messy" problem.

Throughout the process, students work individually and in small collaborative groups around varying problem strands. With the goal of helping students develop flexible thinking and effective problem-solving skills, each team is encouraged to reach a solution from different perspectives. Your role, as the teacher, is to facilitate this process by scaffolding student learning to reduce the cognitive load or mental effort students experience.

A problem-based learning experience can be short—incorporated into an activity—or long, taking an entire unit or the complete school year. A problem can be from one subject solely or it can incorporate multiple disciplines.

When designing a problem-based lesson and thinking about your project's instructional design, inquiry is at the center of both teaching and student learning. The inquiry should be around a real-world condition that mirrors something that students are familiar with or that they may encounter as an expert in their future profession or in life.

Students should be introduced to group processes, identifying roles and dividing work, as well as practicing how to give feedback and evaluate the work of their peers. They are taking on roles of people who work on authentic problems outside of school walls.

As they work through a problem in small groups, students gain knowledge through personal investigation, by asking good questions, and ultimately learn the basics of forming questions and seeking quality answers. Students develop self-directed learning skills, while at the same time they are learning how to learn, no matter how messy it may be.

PROBLEM-BASED LEARNING

Problem-based activities include a variety of different approaches. To provide a framework see figure 8.1.

From a teaching perspective, the problem-based activity provides you with the potential to transcend from a textbook-centered learning approach to a more student-centered approach. Your students are actively engaged in carrying out the learning task, even at times identifying the direction of the task itself, around their own historical interests and connected to the curriculum material.

To maintain engagement and motivation with the problem-based activity, organization and planning is key. Make daily observations to determine if students are on task, working cooperatively, and gaining appropriate understanding around lesson objectives. To help with this, have students write a

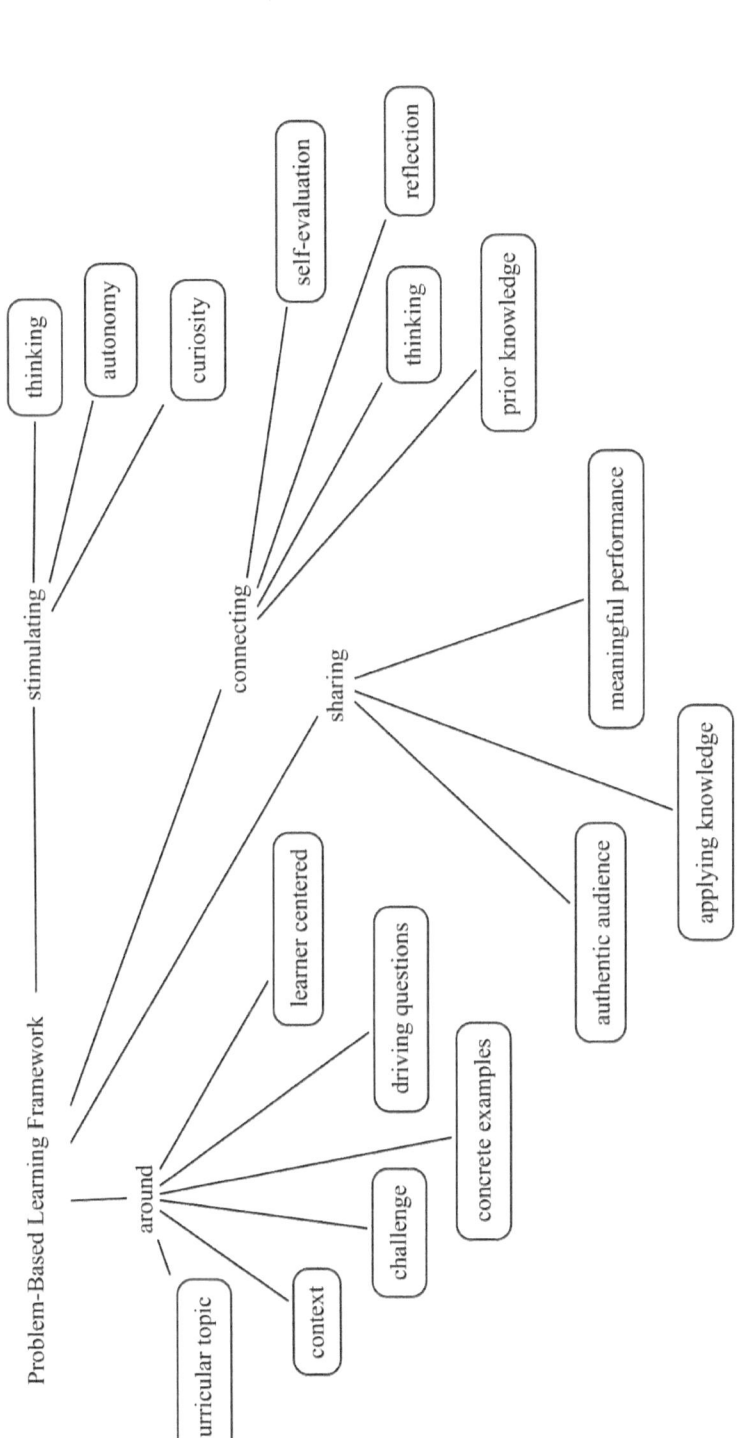

Figure 8.1. Problem-Based Learning Framework

daily journal entry identifying their specific task that day and how their work contributed to the group project as a whole. Collect their journal weekly to provide directed feedback.

At the end of the project, debrief students by reflecting as a group on the project itself and students overall learning. Ask students what worked with the project and what did not. What would they do differently? What would they add? Feedback can be used to improve the activity for next time.

Technology tools should be integrated into the project to help students explore, investigate, and understand the problem so that they begin generating workable solutions. Tools such as word processors, spreadsheets, databases, modeling software and 3D printers, scanners, and/or digital video cameras can be incorporated to provide a real-world element to the project.

You can also provide Internet access and telecommunications so students access relevant and timely information, such as appropriate websites, experts in the field, or e-mail to collect personal accounts. Through this process, students learn how to use technology to work through a real-world problem.

As your students become comfortable working through problem-based activities and identifying solutions, encourage them to build on their innovative thought and ability to move beyond the obvious to a new level of understanding. Innovative thought is what this chapter explores in detail so you can begin creating problem-based activities that will have students producing creative results.

COGNITIVE ENGAGEMENT

The central goal of problem-based learning is cognitive engagement. Meaningful learning requires engagement and the problem focus should help create this. As a teacher, you have seen students procedurally engaged, whereby they wait for you to direct and guide their learning. You present the lesson and students take notes. Later, students demonstrate understanding by taking an end-of-unit test.

For students to be *substantially* and *authentically* engaged, it is important to interact with the content in a deep and thoughtful manner. This can be done with a well-designed problem-based activity, such as the newspaper activity described in figure 8.2. Within this or any problem-based project, peer feedback is encouraged, students reflect on their work, and specific learning goals are carried out.

Problem-based learning is a form of systems thinking and design philosophy. It is a process where students use prior learning, apply it to the whole

In this problem-based activity, students create a historical newspaper.

Students practice writing and research skills, as well as develop presentation skills. In small groups of approximately three to four students, each group selects a historical date or event and a historical city to report on, whether domestic or international.

A telecollaborative activity (see chapter 9) could also be included in the lesson with students from different countries working together to write the newspaper. Students from each country could then compare and contrast the differing views and events.

The task for this problem-based lesson is to design and develop a newspaper that could have been published in a particular city after a specific date or event. In keeping authentic to the time period, students produce a newspaper in historical style and form.

Groups select a name for their newspaper and each group is responsible for maintaining the authenticity of the design to include text and images.

Each group member selects a particular content area or section of the newspaper to write and present, whether in written or pictorial form. This can include the main story, world news, local or regional news, music, sports, science, advertisements, and so on.

In order to write and present the newspaper section, students conduct research by reviewing primary source documents and then edit their work in preparation for peer review.

During the formative evaluation of their peers, feedback is provided on the content and presentation of each group member's work. Once completed, copies are distributed to the teacher, library, and other peer groups.

At the conclusion of the project, each group presents a poster session that represents their contributions to the project. Each team can bring in historical artifacts or develop a replica of an artifact. Groups interact with the poster presentation and the class learns more about a given time period or event.

An evaluation rubric that identifies the key areas of assessment—historical research, writing, collaborative work, design and production, and whole class presentation—can be created and utilized.

The activity is open-ended, for example, students can select any noteworthy event and corresponding city location that interests them, but planning is necessary to ensure students receive clear guidelines of each intended expectation.

The following guidelines are helpful in the planning process:

- Establish project time frame (to include during class and overall project completion).

(continued)

Figure 8.2. Problem-Based Activity Example

- Determine the group selection process.
- Prepare an assessment rubric.
- Select events and time period (groups work on different events and/or time periods).
- Determine topic selection (do students choose their topic or do you?).
- Evaluate research (specify types of research used to find information).
- Decide length of newspaper project (e.g., three to four pages).
- Provide poster presentation guidelines (critical elements to be covered).

Figure 8.2. (*continued*)

system, and then identify multiple relationships with its many distinct parts. Nothing can be focused on in isolation. A holistic view must be taken.

The main idea of problem-based learning is that students produce more self-efficacy in their knowledge construction and as a result have the potential to apply deeper awareness through a range of cognitive meanings. They can then apply these new meanings by transferring them to new situations.

By encouraging students to experiment with ideas, allowing opportunities to learn from mistakes, and helping them to develop skills to work through difficult challenges and tasks, you set the stage for students to become more self-reliant and purposeful in their learning. As the teacher, you provide constructive, directed feedback and help students build upon their abilities to reason at a higher level and to become an innovative thinker in the process.

PLANNING FOR PROBLEM-BASED LEARNING

To entice and motivate students to work on a specific problem, such as cleaning up a polluted stream running through their town or to design specific steps that can be taken to save an endangered species, you must have a well-designed problem.

When designing the problem, it is preferable to allow students choice of topic and content of the finished product. This allows them to incorporate their own interests into the activity thereby facilitating motivation as well as encouraging deeper understanding.

In developing a successful problem-based activity, consider your students, the course content, technology integration, as well as the problem itself. Figure 8.3 looks at each of these areas in more detail.

In designing your problem-based activity, ensure that students have the background knowledge around the topic being studied. Short and simple projects work best when first beginning this type of project. Initially, all

Engaging in Problem-Based Learning   87

Students:
What are their interests and concerns?
What applicable issues are facing your local community? The world as a whole?
  How does the issue(s) relate to students?

Content:
What are the major curriculum standards to be addressed?
What are your curricular goals?
What is the "big idea" you want students to understand?

Methodology:
What is the problem and current situation?
Where is the location of the problem, for example, is it local, national, or global?
How does the project fit into the overall big idea of the curricular subject?
What is the intended purpose of the project? Is there a consequence to students?
Who is the intended audience?

Technology:
What technology resources are available to you?
How accessible is the technology support and/or training?
Which technology tools can be incorporated?

Figure 8.3. Planning for Problem-Based Learning

students can be working on the same tasks in the same order. As students develop skills, more autonomy can be provided. Autonomy is applied by taking more initiative or by defining the scope and goals of a specific part of the project.

Tasks can also be identified according to a specific timeline and problem parts broken down into manageable sections. The problem-based activity incorporates authentic elements, is challenging, and is student-centered, whereby students are in more control of their own learning around the subject. They are working collaboratively in groups with the expectation of solving an open-ended problem.

STEP-BY-STEP PROCESS OF PROBLEM SOLVING

There is a distinct, instructional flow that takes place as students work through a problem (see figure 8.4).

It begins with *exploration*. This first step requires students to develop cognitive structures, such as identifying specific patterns or relationships that apply to the particular problem. In this initial exploratory stage, provide students with concrete examples, such as materials they can touch, see, smell, taste, or

88   *Chapter Eight*

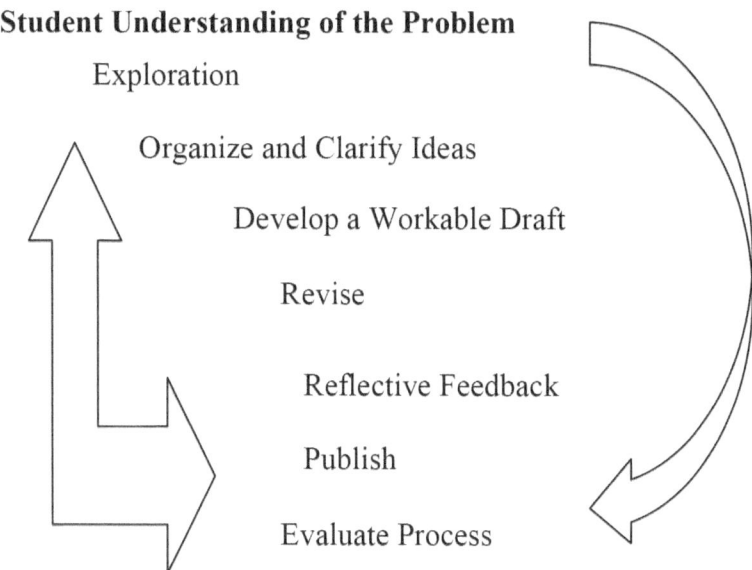

Figure 8.4. Step-by-Step Problem-Based Activity Process

interact with. Engage students in questions and comments. Have them share ideas and overall curiosity with the content. What are they observing?

The next step is to *organize and clarify ideas*. Students make connections with their prior knowledge by organizing, describing, and clarifying with one another what they noticed and any specific questions or concerns. Have students log these connections and concerns by drawing or writing information. Have students make abstract generalizations to find patterns or formulate rules.

Identify ways students can deliberate about their learning. Metacognition can be integrated throughout the problem-based project with activities such as journaling, discussion and self-evaluation, and receiving peer feedback. This provides cognitive validation to ensure student judgment as well as understanding.

You can also begin assessing knowledge through formative assessment almost immediately. Continually facilitate student learning throughout the problem scenario with built-in iterations of information processing. By observing student acquisition of knowledge and skills obtained, with the inclusion of self-reflection and constant monitoring, you can assess the level of interaction with the material and the learning taking place. Notice what words students are using to identify and think about the problem.

This greatly helps you determine level of understanding as they move into the third stage which is to *develop a workable draft*. During this stage, students begin sharing evidence of what was learned by analyzing and integrating information and then applying this information into their new paradigm of understanding. Ensure that you provide quality time for students to work with the material and help them develop their findings to demonstrate new knowledge gained in their own words.

Transitioning to the next stage occurs when students are able to explain and *revise* their understanding. As the teacher, you clarify knowledge gained by building on student descriptions with new information. Pace your content and the skills necessary for students to obtain during this process so students enjoy the challenge and are comfortable revising their work as needed.

During the *reflective stage*, encourage students' cognitive, physical, and emotional engagement by presenting the material in multiple ways to meet the diverse needs and understanding of your students. Your goal is to ensure that the information is relevant so they want to learn and work with new material.

Questioning continues during this step. Encourage students to question both within groups and individually. Encourage students to apply their new knowledge to their own life or the world around them by doing something relevant that will influence change without imitating something someone else has already done, such as what you originally presented.

As the teacher, model good questions for students to ask during this step. Model curiosity and react positively to student questions, guiding them to develop even deeper questions. How you interact with students during each of these stages determines how engaged they are throughout the problem-based activity process.

Have students do something to *publish* their results. Write a letter, make a phone call, send an e-mail, interview experts, or conduct research on the Internet. Encourage them to be creative to demonstrate understanding by writing a report, a journal, a letter, preparing an editorial, or role playing. They could use animation, a movie, poster, model, or teach what they have learned to others. During this stage, your role is to build on student strengths, thereby enhancing their learning. Technology integration is also encouraged at this presentation stage.

The final stage is *evaluation*. This is where both the student and the teacher reflect on the effectiveness of the lesson. Final questions include

- What sense did I make of this activity?
- What could I have done differently?

- How do I know that I learned a new skill or have new knowledge?
- How will I use this new information moving forward and in my everyday life?

TWENTY-FIRST-CENTURY SKILLS AND TECHNOLOGY INTEGRATION

When utilizing a problem-based learning approach, view technology integration as a seamless link to the work and learning students will do throughout the problem-solving process, as well as to motivate and inspire them.

Include twenty-first-century skills, such as those embodied in the National Educational Technology Standards for Students (NETs) developed through the International Society of Technology Education (ISTE). Discussed in chapter 4, these include skills such as creativity and innovation, communication and collaboration, research and information fluency, critical thinking, problem solving, and decision making, as well as digital citizenship, and technology operations and concepts.

NETs, along with the technology integration models introduced in chapter 4 (the Technology Integration Matrix, TPACK, and SAMR), help provide good indicators that you can use to focus your project design around the necessary skills and knowledge that students must demonstrate once they complete the project, as well as ensure that the technology integrated is used as a cognitive tool.

SUMMARY

Inquiry-based teaching is a pedagogical approach that uses strategies and methods that provide rich opportunities for students to discover and explore content around an authentic problem.

By incorporating a problem into your lesson, students move beyond basic subject mastery to more content mastery and sophisticated thinking about real-world skills and knowledge. The goal is to ask questions that demand higher level thinking beyond factual information, providing opportunities for students to think critically and to analyze information and ideas.

The problem revolves around curriculum standards and can help students see the "big picture" of your curriculum or specific content area. If you include interdisciplinary topics, your students receive an even broader view of the world around them and how information and ideas are connected.

Ensure that enough time is given to research the problem, review one another's work, and provide constructive feedback. Technology tools should be incorporated as a cognitive tool and used seamlessly throughout the problem-based activity.

A goal of a problem-based learning activity, beyond learning your intended outcome, is for each student to make proficient progress toward becoming an independent and creative learner that goes beyond knowing basic, factual information.

REFLECTION

1. Problem-based learning is a model where students are engaged in an authentic problem, scenario, or challenge around your curriculum goals. How would you use a step-by-step process when designing your problem-based lesson?
2. How does problem-based learning help to develop content knowledge as well as problem-solving strategies and skills?
3. In your inquiry design, what are some ways you can encourage self-directed learning?
4. Demonstrate how technology can be used as an authentic, as well as a cognitive, tool in the problem-solving process.
5. Identify key areas related to problem-based learning to add to your inquiry framework.

SKILL BUILDING ACTIVITY

Throughout this chapter, emphasis was placed on problem-based learning and how it aligns your learning goals around an authentic problem. Now you can begin thinking about how to incorporate a problem, scenario, or concern into your inquiry lesson. Follow the steps below to get started:

- From your identified problem that aligns with your learning standards, create a lesson that incorporates specific scaffolding activities to help facilitate and guide students' problem solving and inquiry.
- Provide ways for students to connect with other subjects in your problem (at least one). Whether you use resources, ideas, or even part of the problem-solving activity, require information from at least one other subject or discipline to complete the activity.

- Identify technology tools that aid in supporting student thinking with research and analysis, as well as information sharing through collaboration with other students.
- Identify outcomes that you expect students to demonstrate and some possible ways they can be demonstrated.

Chapter Nine

Global Connections and Telecollaborative Learning

As you and your team have been working on your inquiry-based project, you have identified multiple ways to incorporate twenty-first-century skills. In your last faculty meeting, the principal, Ms. Leeds, additionally began discussing the need for faculty to incorporate more global connections into courses.

She mentioned the potential of telecollaborative activities and some ways in which this approach could be integrated into the inquiry learning experience so students would be able to reach a deeper understanding of the course content by building connections to the outside world.

You and your team decide to investigate telecollaborative learning, specifically how you will incorporate this into your inquiry unit. You decide to investigate the possibilities further.... There is a lot to consider.

Before your next meeting, you and your team need to decide which type of telecollaborative activity you want to implement into the inquiry unit.

Telecollaborative learning provides opportunities for students to work as a collaborative group with others outside of the classroom and at a distance around curricular goals using communication technologies. Others outside of the classroom can include experts in the field or even classes in other states or countries.

Any telecommunications tool can be utilized for a telecollaborative activity. The Internet is perhaps the best known and it provides a dynamic environment due to its vast resources and tools that are simple to use. More importantly, the Internet provides access to classrooms and experts around the world on issues that are authentic and timely to students and the overall curriculum. A telecollaborative activity combines the benefit of the Internet with the collaboration and sharing of information at a distance.

When you integrate a telecollaborative activity into your classroom, you are providing opportunities for students to connect with your intended learning goals by actively participating with others outside of the classroom around a curricular topic to solve a problem, answer a question, or create something new.

In this chapter, telecollaborative activities are explored. Your class can either join a telecollaborative activity or you can create one and invite other classes to participate. Either way, telecollaboration is a relevant learning experience for you and your students. See figure 9.1 for a framework to help you design a telecollaborative activity.

TELECOLLABORATIVE ACTIVITIES

A telecollaborative activity provides opportunities for students to work and create information with other students or experts in different geographical locations using online communication tools. These digital tools can be text based and asynchronous or video based and synchronous.

Tools can range from e-mail, blogs, wikis, Skype, Google Hangouts, VoiceThread, to Twitter, just to name a few. Any digital tool connected to the Internet that provides opportunities for discussion, debate, and the potential for intercultural interchange can be used. Locations can be as close as down the hall or as far away as around the world.

The benefits of telecollaborative activities are the ability to connect through the Internet with other students, teachers, researchers, scientists, politicians, and business leaders throughout the globe around important issues that relate to your learning goals.

Telecollaborative activities are curriculum based, and teacher designed and coordinated. Most have websites to share information collected and information about the activity itself. A telecollaborative activity is usually integrated directly into the curriculum and is not an extra activity.

As with any inquiry-oriented activity, your goal as the teacher is to engage students with an essential question and then let them discover workable answers. The only difference between a telecollaborative activity and other inquiry-oriented activities is the opportunity for students to work with other students and/or experts in the field around the world on these authentic and meaningful problems that have been identified in the inquiry activity.

For example, a telecollaborative activity can be designed for students to collect raw data, such as weather data in their community or to identify family eating habits. Once the data is collected, they then post it into an online database.

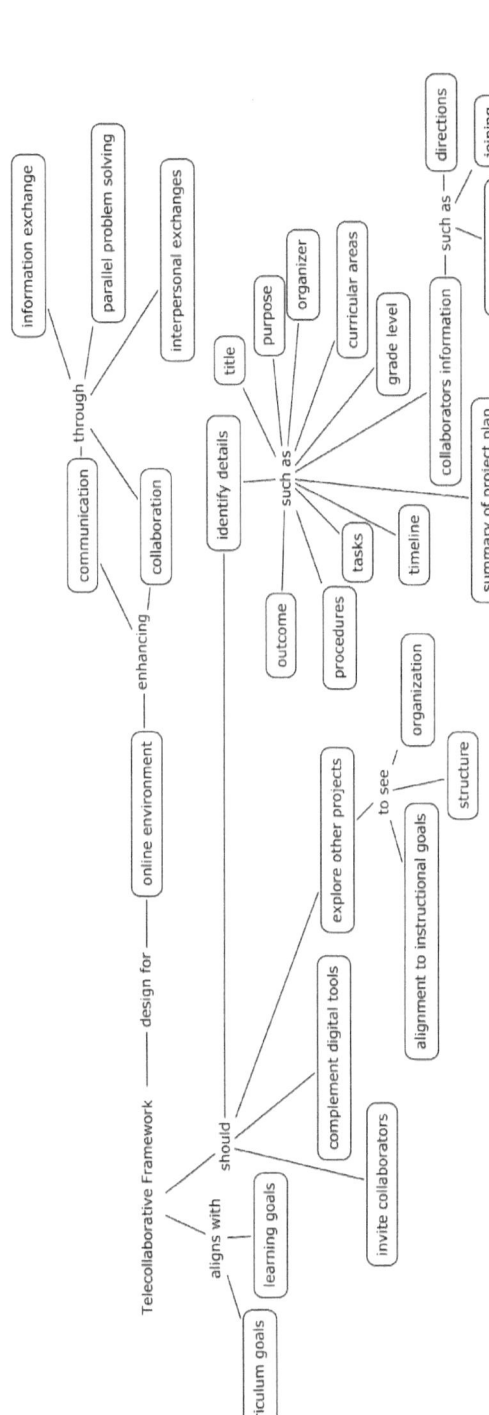

Figure 9.1. Telecollaborative Framework

As each class posts their information, other students and/or experts now have the ability to access all the inputted data and interact with the information to help solve the identified problem. Students can share their findings with the collected group for discussion and debate. See figure 9.2 for a more detailed example of a telecollaborative activity.

You are planning a unit on the Revolutionary War in your social studies class.

A typical lesson on this unit would have students read a chapter on the Revolutionary War, then go to the library to find further information on this historical event, and prepare a written report for class.

An enhancement to this activity could include a telecollaborative element by having students work with another class in a different part of the world. This would provide an opportunity for intercultural and information exchange around issues of conflict and change.

You would begin by

- Identifying how your essential question relates to this activity and begin identifying subquestions. Each question is developed to engage students to think about broad issues.
- Explaining how interacting with a class or experts from outside of your school can help students with their quest in finding answers.
- Collecting primary source documents to help prepare students with their inquiry activity, such as letters, images, papers, and/or maps.
- Planning your instruction, identifying a timeline, providing benchmarks for assignments, and selecting a debate topic.
- Contacting teachers through a telecollaborative service (e.g., ePals) to see who might be interested.

A teacher from England responds to your inquiry, agreeing to a classroom debate, and a question is established:

Could a compromise have been reached before the Revolutionary War began? If so, how would the result of the compromise have changed the course of history?

Students receive a unique experience tackling this curriculum topic from a variety of perspectives through primary research, identifying an argument, debating, using the Internet as a tool for learning, all with another class from England who may have a different viewpoint of the war and the results. This type of activity offers both classes a distinct perspective of this event in history from varying locations and cultural perspectives.

The varying perspectives and resources submitted from both classes as well as the awe of the long distance link are noteworthy. Information from the classroom debate can be collected on a wiki page where both classes can add to the information and make changes. In addition, lessons learned can be documented as well as offering the potential for ongoing dialog with this international classroom.

Figure 9.2. Telecollaborative Activity Example

COMPUTER TECHNOLOGIES AND THE INTERNET

When incorporating telecollaboration into your classroom, the Internet is the central telecommunications tool due to its ability to bridge classes and experts, allowing each to share information and ideas using a variety of tools. Your goal is to identify tools that allow you and your students to communicate by sharing and exchanging information.

There are many telecommunication tools that can facilitate a telecollaborative exchange. These include platform tools such as Edmodo, Wikispaces, Wordpress, or Weebly; online presentation tools such as Prezi, Fotobable, Google Slides, or VoiceThread; communication tools such as those allowing communication in real time using Skype, Google Hangouts, or asynchronously at different times, such as forums or e-mail using tools such as Eyejot, MailVu, or even using the recording feature in VoiceThread.

As you begin identifying tools, you then need to determine which ones you have available to you, the skill level needed, and how the tool will best help students achieve the intended learning goals as well as continue their development with digital and information literacy and technology fluency.

When joining a telecollaborative activity developed by another teacher, you need to tailor the activity to your curricular goals and standards, but you also want to ensure that the tools that you have available meet the needs of the other classroom or participants.

COLLABORATIVE INTERACTIONS

There are a variety of telecollaborative activities that you and your class can participate in. One is a *global classroom*. A global classroom is a collaborative environment that uses the Internet and a variety of digital tools, to include communication and collaboration, to open the classroom up to outside organizations and interests around curricular goals.

The classroom is constructive in nature and produces a complex learning experience. Students explore course topics centered around authentic problems and engage in active participation by posting and manipulating documents and data, and/or by communicating through e-mail or chatting with others around the globe.

As a collective group, the problem is solved and questions answered. An example of a global classroom can be found at the United Nations Global Classroom project. This website provides dynamic opportunities for middle and high school students worldwide to explore current global issues as a collective group.

Another type of telecollaborative learning opportunity is an *electronic appearance* that is usually led and conducted by an expert in the field. You could have an author of the book that you are reading communicate with your students via Skype so your students can ask questions or learn more about character development. Or you could have a scientist dial into your class when your students present their newly created 3D models so the expert scientist can ask questions or add new information or insights.

Electronic mentoring is another type of telecollaborative opportunity that allows students to ask questions of an expert from industry or business. Students direct questions around their own research. The goal is to get more information to help work through an identified problem. The experts assist in directing student research and questioning. Electronic mentoring can come from sites such as Ask an Expert or the MadSci Network.

In each of these telecollaborative interactions, communication around specific topics as well as working with others, including experts in the field and at a distance, are the central focus. There are many ways students can interact with others outside of class. For example, to communicate and exchange information with a wide audience, students can create a website, attach files to e-mail, use a cloud service to store and transfer files from one participant to another, input data into an online database, or use conferencing tools that are cross platform.

There are also variations in the type of communication methods as shown below from which students convey meaning to the data collected and the information analyzed:

- Written format, such as letters, poems, storyboards, and stories
- Data analysis using spreadsheets, graphs, and charts
- Visually with images, sketches, and artwork
- Auditory with narration and music
- Multimedia, combining each of the above elements, plus animation

The only requirement is that whichever method(s) you choose, it must meet the needs of your learners, learning goals, and participants. Figure 9.3 provides an overview of the cooperation intended in a telecollaborative activity.

PREPARATION AND PLANNING FOR YOUR TELECOLLABORATIVE ACTIVITY

In a telecollaborative activity, students work on similar activities in different locations, cultures, and time zones. This is a major strength of this inquiry-

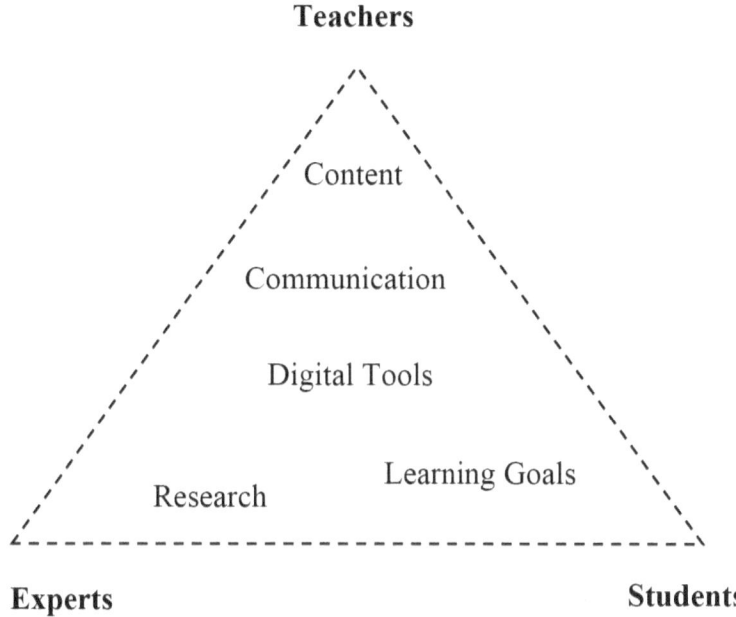

Figure 9.3. Cooperative Interactions

oriented activity, but it requires planning and specific benchmarks to accomplish your goals.

To help prepare, ensure that your specific benchmark dates as well as your reflection and feedback opportunities are varied and manageable. This assists students and/or experts at each location in collecting and sharing information online so that the information is available for all participants to analyze and evaluate due to time zones and/or other responsibilities. For example, a class in the United States will be in a different time zone than a class in Japan. How will you work with this time difference or will this even be a concern?

Figure 9.4 demonstrates the opportunity for global thinking through collaboration presented through a telecollaborative activity. In the example, your students, along with students from around the globe, help scientists collect data. They have a direct impact on the outcome of the research and are working alongside real-world scientists and researchers at leading organizations.

In order to participate in a telecollaborative activity, a meaningful project that meets curriculum needs must be offered and Internet access is a requirement. In addition, digital tools to help students analyze, communicate, manipulate, synthesize, and share information (such as spreadsheet, word processing, e-mail, video conferencing, and presentation tools) are also needed.

> In a science class, your goal is to have students think locally as well as globally about the environment and earth systems.
>
> In deciding on a telecollaborative activity, you begin by conducting an Internet search and find a resource at the Global Learning and Observations to Benefit the Environment (GLOBE) website.
>
> After reviewing the GLOBE website, you become aware that teachers and students from around the world are already conducting primary research and collaborating with scientists from both the National Aeronautics and Space Administration (NASA) and the National Science Association (NSA). You are excited to have your class participate.
>
> As part of the project, you work with your students to collect quality data in your local area on a specific plant and animal group that is outlined on the GLOBE website. Once your class collects the appropriate primary data, they import the information into the GLOBE database.
>
> There are specific benchmarks that must be met so the data can be used by classrooms around the world as well as by NASA and NSA scientists to create a satellite map of specific animal and plant populations around the world.
>
> The information your students collect and upload into the database is then used as primary research by scientists in these two organizations.

Figure 9.4. Global Thinking through Collaboration

Start by providing students with a relevant problem that is real world and purposeful, and one that can be investigated. Next, explore other classrooms and inquire with experts interested in participating.

Planning is important so students can explore the content provided in the telecollaborative activity in relation to the curriculum and learning goals, and then can share their information and experiences with other participating classrooms. Planning involves identifying specific learning objectives and goals for your class, such as practicing conversational Spanish or identifying similarities and differences among cultures and peoples.

It also includes setting clear benchmarks for due dates and identified tasks, such as collecting and sharing information among the class and with the telecollaborative partners. In addition, planning time is also spent finding a topic and identifying a specific product that engages students and increases their understanding of your content area around a real-world context.

When starting the planning process, first begin by looking at your curriculum. Start by outlining course topics and then determining major themes that you will be covering throughout the academic year. As you identify main topics and key themes, ideas for a telecollaborative activity that your class

Alignment with the Telecollaborative Activity

- Curriculum and Learning Goals &
- Technology Tools and Capabilites

Project Design and Collaboration

- Identify Lesson Details (specific activities to complete, timeline, procedures, collaborations) &
- Seek Collaborators (send out lesson on telecollaborative Web sites)

Complement Digital Tools

- Interpersonal Exchange (use Skype, Google Hangouts, email, Discussion forum)
- Information Exchange (use Project Weblog, Wiki, VoiceThread)
- Time zones will aid in choosing your tool (synchronous versus asynchronous)

Figure 9.5. Telecollaborative Planning Process

can participate in or that you can create for students should become clearer. Planning always begins by looking at your curriculum and identifying major themes and expected outcomes.

Within the telecollaborative activity, interactions must be prepared ahead of time to ensure students have opportunities for meaningful communication that includes discussion and discourse. This means that experts and/or other classrooms need to know when benchmarks have been set for assignments and tasks so they too can coordinate and plan.

When working with others outside of your classroom, another consideration is when and how each member involved in the activity will share and discuss due to possible time conflicts. There is a lot to consider when planning. Figure 9.5 provides an overview of the planning process for your telecollaborative activity.

Start Small

When you first begin a telecollaborative activity, it is best to start small. For example, consider exploring an activity that involves using e-mail to exchange a message or to share information about your community or class.

As an illustration, the Global Grocery Project lets students collect data and add their own data to an online database that records local grocery prices. You can then use the data in this database to incorporate into math problems.

These types of introductory activities allow you and your students to experience a telecollaborative activity without an extensive time or resource commitment. Once you and your students become comfortable collecting and sharing information, you can grow to larger and more involved activities.

When first starting out, it is also helpful to find another teacher at your school that wants to participate. Another option is to include your technology resource teacher. It is important to have assistance, especially with larger and more involved projects, and to know what resources you need and what you have available for use. If you are missing something, can you manage? And if not, you need to determine how you will obtain the necessary resources to be successful.

It is important to identify your technology skill level and determine what support you need to complete the activity. Do not be afraid to ask for help. Your technology resource teacher is an excellent resource. Remember that other classrooms are counting on the data that students collect and share, so make sure that you are prepared and have the necessary assistance to be successful.

INCORPORATING INQUIRY INTO TELECOLLABORATIVE ACTIVITIES

Once you have determined the types and methods of communication, and established the planning process, the next step is to identify inquiry activities for students that tie into a specific learning goal. There are various types of inquiry-oriented activities that can be integrated into a telecollaborative activity.

For example, information collection and analysis allows students to collect, compare, contrast, and synthesize complex information they have collected and evaluated. This information can be posted for other classrooms around the world to access and evaluate.

Generally, information *collection and analysis* involves an online database that can be accessed by all and queried. This information can then be used to think more innovatively about a problem, coming up with a creative solution.

Problem-solving activities can also be used. This provides students with a complex, ill-structured problem that encourages them to critically analyze and synthesize information. This information can use primary and secondary information, from which students present innovative solutions.

Types of problem-solving activities include social action projects, peer feedback activities, and information exchanges. In each type, students examine a problem, such as high gas prices, and then use data to determine the best solution for stakeholders, in this case both the local and global economy.

Whether students are collecting and analyzing information or problem solving, your role as the teacher is to encourage and guide them throughout the process. You provide varied and engaging opportunities for students to research appropriate resources and compile real-world data so others (e.g., experts in the field) can use this information along with your students to help determine possible solutions.

In each learning opportunity presented in a telecollaborative activity, students practice digital literacy and information literacy skills. Students explore relevant topics and conduct research to find answers to specific questions.

Students practice information-seeking and information-evaluating skills. Information seeking is when students investigate and explore topics using research methods. Information evaluating is when students evaluate found information to make sure it is reliable and valid.

Telecollaborative activities typically focus on information exchange and data collection, both of which provide opportunities for knowledge sharing and allow students to gather, analyze, and compare information.

DESIGNING AND EVALUATING YOUR OWN TELECOLLABORATIVE ACTIVITY

As you begin the design process for your own telecollaborative activity, start by researching existing projects to give you ideas. During the planning and development phase, be mindful that you are writing for fellow teachers, not students. Peer teachers will review the activity guidelines and expectations to determine if they want their class to participate in your project.

During the initial design period, identify possible participants, such as earth science or English literature classes. Establishing cocurricular projects can be beneficial for you and your students, so consider these cross-curricular opportunities as well.

You do not necessarily have to work with classes in your same subject area and can branch out to other disciplines to incorporate more dynamic data and subsequent findings. Figure 9.6 outlines some useful guidelines for designing your telecollaborative activity.

> 1. Identify your learning goals and objectives.
> 2. Ensure that the implementation of the activity is straightforward and that it can continue throughout its duration.
> 3. Confirm that the activity is appropriate for the chosen digital tools and the type of learning.
> 4. Involve students throughout the activity with ample opportunity for hands-on experience.
> 5. Collaborate with other classes, schools, or experts in the field. Build in opportunities for continued communication with participants.
> 6. Clearly and specifically identify how each participant will communicate and exchange information.
> 7. Provide a clear and doable timeline that includes specific benchmarks for each participant for the duration of the project.
> 8. Include continuous and appropriate student assessment and evaluation throughout the activity.
> 9. Communicate in a timely manner to all participants regarding the closing date of the project and the results of the data obtained once compiled and evaluated.

Figure 9.6. Guidelines for Designing Your Own Telecollaborative Activity

Once these guidelines have been met, prepare your project goals, topic, theme, and requirements. Make sure that the information is well-defined for all participants to follow.

Next, determine how you will compile and distribute the results to the participants once the activity has concluded. And finally, identify both formal and informal methods of evaluation of student work.

Ensure that you have enough participants for your activity to gather suitable data. Some will drop out or not submit all data sets, so ensure your activity is long enough and has enough participants to pull good information from your data. Conversely, if your activity has too many participants, this can also be a problem. Strive for a balance.

As you work with other participants, make sure to maintain continued and open contact. Meet all set deadlines and remind participants of deadlines and benchmarks. Motivate your students as well as the other participants by letting them know that this is an important activity and the work that they are doing is meaningful and worth the effort.

Be flexible. We all have technology issues and may not be aware of these issues when we begin the activity. Ensure that you have the technical support needed to answer questions and help with alternative solutions if need be.

After developing and creating a telecollaborative activity, it is important to review to ensure you are meeting course learning goals and utilizing the collaboration and communication tools available to you. In evaluating your activity, confirm that

- The activity aligns with the appropriate learning expectations;
- It is realistic and doable;
- Activities are clearly outlined and appropriately sequenced; and
- Appropriate benchmarks and deadlines are identified.

SUMMARY

Telecollaborative activities use the Internet and digital technologies to collaborate and communicate with others around the globe on a curricular topic. Your goal is to use the power of the Internet and other technology tools to engage learners in the project by working with one another as well as experts in the field.

Telecollaborative projects present a very effective learning model for inquiry learning. They provide an opportunity for students to conduct real-world work around curricular goals with people both inside and outside of your classroom, oftentimes providing differing perspectives as well as locations.

REFLECTION

1. As you think about integrating telecollaborative activities into your inquiry lesson, remember to start small and then grow in difficulty and involvement. Do an Internet search on telecollaborative activities and look at some examples. What did you find? Which ones interested you? Which ones did not and why? What are some simple telecollaborative activities that you could incorporate into your inquiry lesson to engage students to think differently?
2. After you had an opportunity to explore less complex telecollaborative activities, it is time to investigate more involved activities. What is the difference between a simple activity and a more complex telecollaborative activity? How could a more involved activity be incorporated into your inquiry lesson? How would it engage your learners with your learning goals? How would it help your students to experience global learning?

SKILL BUILDING ACTIVITY

Create your own telecollaborative project. Identify learning standards, topics, and resources. Next, determine what activities will help students meet each of the learning goals using telecommunication tools. Document your activity and begin seeking participants.

Post on a telecollaborative listserv, such as Classroom Projects or post your activity on services such as ePals or KidLink. Make sure that your telecollaborative activity encourages students to dig deeper into your problem and develop a greater understanding of your learning goals for the lesson.

Chapter Ten

Using Technologies for Assessment and Feedback

In preparing for your next team meeting, you have identified components of a good lesson, such as standards, an essential question and subquestions, as well as learning outcomes. Just recently you identified a meaningful problem to ensure that learning is relevant for your students, but what about assessments that are authentic?

At this point, it is time for you and your team to think more concretely about how you will use technology tools to assess student learning. You have been contemplating the following questions:

- An authentic assessment includes a task for students to perform and a rubric to evaluate their performance. What type of task should your students perform and how will this task complement your inquiry unit?
- What types of technology tools will both engage students in their learning and allow them to perform effectively and creatively throughout the assessment?

Each team member has agreed to research the above two questions and then discuss them at your next team meeting to help design the authentic assessment for your inquiry project. What are your thoughts?

As you have discovered throughout this book, inquiry involves asking an essential question coupled with subquestions to guide students through an authentic problem or situation found in the real world. Throughout this process, students use diverse media, resources, and digital tools to provide stronger connections to the content, their peers, and outside experts. All of this is accomplished so students think more deeply about the content and how it relates to their authentic experiences.

When focusing learning tasks on authentic problems, authentic assessments can help determine student learning and understanding. An authentic assessment is defined as a realistic task that requires judgment, innovation, and asks students to do a specific activity to demonstrate understanding. As with the inquiry lesson, it replicates or simulates a real-world skill and allows students to rehearse, practice, use relevant resources and media, reflect on their learning, and receive feedback during the assessment.

Each inquiry-oriented activity explored throughout this text focuses on creating authentic experiences using the process of active discovery and exploration around good questions. As such, it is important to consider the integrated challenge of incorporating authentic assessments requiring a range of skills and knowledge, as well as the use of digital tools in an authentic manner, to assess student learning.

An authentic assessment framework is shown in figure 10.1. This framework lays out a plan of action for utilizing authentic assessments in your inquiry activity to assess student learning, as well as improve skills and overall understanding.

AUTHENTIC ASSESSMENTS

When you think of an authentic assessment, think of learning. Authentic assessments are designed around learning goals and measure student knowledge as well as the ability to apply new understanding in new and authentic ways. Authentic assessments should be continuous and embedded seamlessly throughout instruction in order to provide you and your students with information about their learning and your instruction.

Once it is identified what students must do to demonstrate mastery, you can determine if an authentic assessment will help assess this level of mastery. Think of including an *authentic* assessment when you want to resemble tasks and experiences completed in the real world and students can demonstrate thinking and learning by applying, reflecting, and creating a product or performance.

An authentic assessment can be aligned with multiple learning tasks, such as the ability to

- Communicate clearly,
- Participate actively in groups,
- Comprehend reading,
- Conduct an experiment,
- Classify ideas, and
- Make judgments and comparisons.

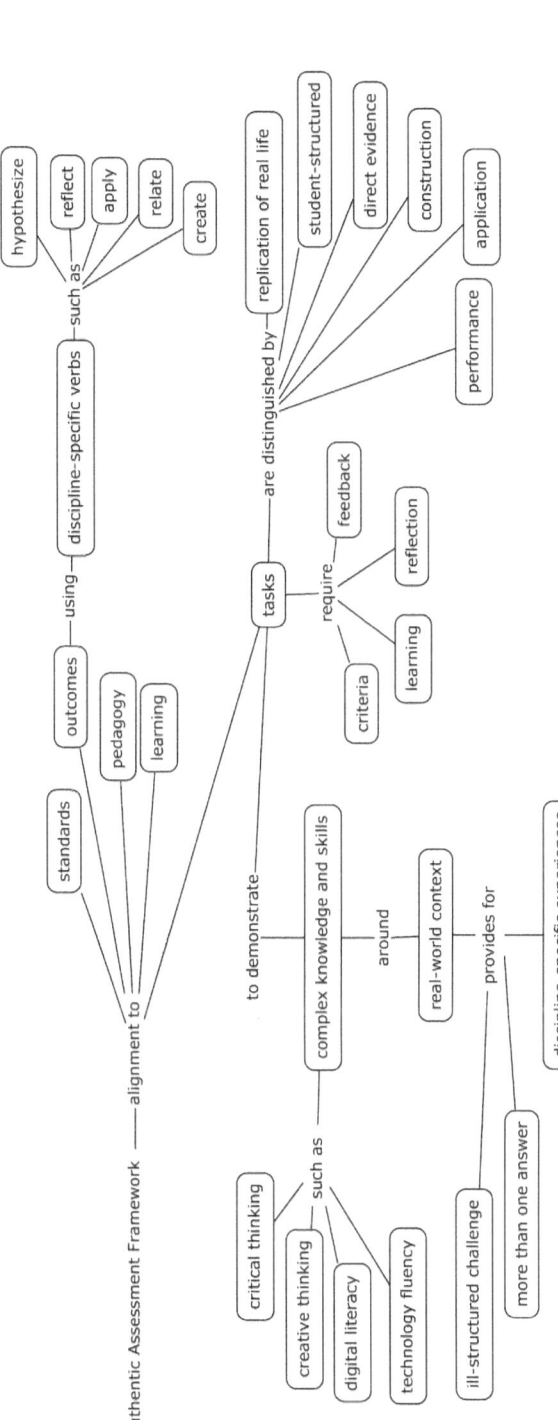

Figure 10.1. Authentic Assessment Framework

In science class, students are studying endangered animals and they have just finished exploring the ecosystem of the Amazon rain forest. You want to assess what has been learned before you move on to the next lesson.

You choose an essential question to focus student thinking around the final product for the assessment:

Why is there conflict in the rain forest?

Instruction was given to students to work in small groups to create a 30-second public service announcement (PSA) that introduces the main themes discovered in the lesson. These themes include

- people
- endangered animals
- adaptations
- change

You set the audience as their parents and other classmates because you want the audience to pose questions and comments to each group's PSA.

To be successful, each individual student needs a comprehensive understanding of each of the themes, such that he or she has made connections with the research and how the various themes relate to the current conflict occurring in the rain forest. From this individual compilation of data and information, students integrate their notes within their peer group.

The final project delivery comprises each group posting their commercial (PSA) onto the class blog with a five-sentence paragraph that provides a brief description of the problem and introduces how their PSA answers the essential question. Following execution of the PSA, each group will also encourage discussion and debate from the audience that they then respond to.

This authentic assessment allows for a blended design, for example, both online and face-to-face instruction.

In class, groups complete a storyboard and script and then compile their images and text into a 30-second PSA video. The video and five-sentence paragraph introduction is then placed onto the class weblog. As part of the final assessment, students are also tasked with reviewing other teams' PSAs and providing an online discussion reflection and response.

In evaluating this assessment, it is important to provide a rubric with criterion and descriptors that can be utilized by students to help guide them through key elements needed to demonstrate mastery.

This is an authentic assessment in that it can be done in the real world and students can demonstrate knowledge and skills by applying what they learned.

Figure 10.2.   Authentic Assessment Example

So what does an authentic assessment look like? See an example in figure 10.2.

The difference between a traditional and authentic assessment is that when students are presented with a problem in an authentic assessment they utilize the knowledge and skills gained during the unit to decipher and solve the problem. They also continue to learn throughout the assessment with you, the teacher, facilitating that process.

In this manner, the process of learning is just as important as the final outcome. An authentic assessment focuses on how students meaningfully applied the concepts of the unit, rather than just a drill-and-practice exercise to ensure they can remember facts, as in a traditional assessment.

Evidence of learning can take many forms, such as short-answer essays, graphing limericks, creating concept maps, peer editing, designing an experiment, analyzing or writing a musical composition, designing a reading guide, or creating an infographic of data that identifies the criteria of a problem. There is no standard one-size-fits-all for an authentic assessment.

DESIGNING AN AUTHENTIC ASSESSMENT

Just like the preparation required for an inquiry activity and ultimately an entire learning unit, authentic assessments also take planning as well. Critical and creative thinking are needed to ensure assessments are meaningful and aligned to appropriate tasks.

When designing assessments, clearly identify the expected learning outcome for the unit plan and how this is defined in each lesson. Be sure to outline the vision for your unit and introduce how your essential question(s) for the curriculum is demonstrated.

The unit helps organize instruction and sets learning goals, pacing, and direction. It will identify several standards, skills, and desired learning outcomes. Its purpose is to help organize individual lesson plans into a coherent structure. When examining each unit in your curriculum, a specific journey should be evident and mapped out for students to gain mastery and knowledge.

Throughout the entire unit, you incorporate formative assessments that allow for multiple assessments of student thinking and understanding. At the end of the unit, a culminating performance is presented that relates to the authentic nature of the problem so students can transfer lessons learned and apply what they studied to a meaningful problem.

A lesson plan is more specific and usually designed for a single class period. Each lesson within a unit should contain more specific objectives and learning outcomes, teaching and learning activities, and formative assessments to check for student understanding. It should also incorporate student learning styles and subquestions that help answer identified essential questions for your curricular topic.

Assessments can take a variety of forms such as self-assessments, oral interviews, scenarios or problem-based exercises, exhibitions, writing, experiments, demonstrations, teaching, even teacher observations. Each assessment must align with the specific conditions and parameters identified in the individual lesson and represent the authentic problem that students are working on to solve the problem, issue, or concern.

Lesson objectives help design each assessment and so too do your activities. You are assessing the knowledge and skills needed to carry out the tasks learned throughout the lesson. When designing your inquiry project, ensure that students have opportunities to practice the identified skills and receive feedback so they can then transfer lessons learned into their problem or investigation. Authentic assessments are considered opportunities for students to learn and receive feedback as well as determine each student's understanding of the learning goals.

ASSESSMENT STRATEGIES

Inquiry activities provide opportunities for student learning through engagement. Part of this engagement comes through continued meaningful assessment. Assessments aid both teachers and students by helping them determine if the desired results of the lesson are being achieved.

There are many different assessment strategies that can be used to determine whether students are gaining the necessary information and to ensure that they can move forward with future lessons. As discussed above, assessments take many forms, both informally through observations, questioning techniques, small and large group work, think-pair-share strategies, and more formally through quizzes and project performances.

Informal assessments provide opportunities for you and your students to ask questions. Informal assessments include questions as well as observations. Peer feedback and evaluations are also a form of informal assessment. Informal assessments are not intended to be used for a grade, but instead as a measuring tool to determine student knowledge about a particular concept or idea.

Formal assessments, in contrast, include quizzes, tests, projects, and activities. As the teacher, you provide feedback on these assessments and allow students to ask questions and develop deeper understandings. Other types of assessments include student self-assessments such as portfolios and learning logs.

The key to an effective assessment strategy is to incorporate assessments at the beginning of a unit to determine what students know before instruction begins so you can tailor instruction to meet the needs of every student. Then, additional assessments can be included throughout instruction to ensure students are understanding what is intended.

At the end of the unit, the summative authentic assessment provides a deeper learning experience and an opportunity for students to practice in an applied way the skills and knowledge gained throughout the entire unit.

This form of continued assessment provides opportunities for you, as the teacher, and your students to determine performance and understanding of the topics being explored throughout the learning experience. It provides opportunities to guide students and solicit feedback to help get them on track, if needed, or to surge ahead with an activity.

Assessments should also provide opportunities for students to tie in prior understanding and make personal connections with the topics being explored. As the learning activity continues and students connect their personal interests and prior knowledge to their learning, students can develop deeper cognitive connections.

With each step, you are guiding students through the process of inquiry using questions and instructional problems as a learning tool. These learning tools are also considered forms of assessment. Build on questions, tie in research, and have students continuously share information. With each connection made, you learn more about what students understand.

Entice students to debate with their classmates and if possible, with students from outside the class using Skype, ePals, or Twitter. By incorporating complex learning tasks, such as a debate, students think more concretely about the problem and how their ideas for a solution relate to others.

This is critical and creative thinking, with subsequent presentation, about a problem, the content, and student understanding. Throughout this process, you facilitate the experience to ensure students are on task, engaged, and comprehend what is important. Questions can be used to guide both the inquiry and student learning.

IDENTIFY BENCHMARKS

As students dig deeper and get more involved with the content, they have a richer experience in terms of more profoundly exploring the lesson and discovering new information. Throughout this process, benchmarks or performance tasks are identified to ensure students are on task. As the teacher, you continually evaluate students by having them share their findings with others and outline specifically what they learned by discussing and presenting their findings.

The key to continued assessments is not to wait until the end of an activity to provide feedback to the student, through a summative assessment, but instead to provide measures of performance that involves dynamic and diverse opportunities for reflection and feedback throughout the activity. This helps provide guidance and ensures direction.

It is important to identify concrete benchmarks pulled from your learning goals to outline your tasks. Think of a benchmark as what you want students to understand at specific points during the lesson in order to move onto the next lesson (see figure 10.3).

In tomorrow's math class, the lesson is on seasonal temperatures along a specific latitude and longitude of the atlas. An important component of the lesson is the ability for students to manipulate mathematical models that highlight temperature and climate.

You provide students with an online database, such as worldclimate.com. At this website, up-to-date information and data is stored on temperatures and climates from around the world. Students use this weather database to collect raw data on a particular region of the world and then in collaborative groups they place the data for their specific region into a spreadsheet.

Once student groups place regional weather data in a spreadsheet, the whole class convenes to discuss equations and extract data gathered to answer questions that were identified earlier.

The benchmarks for this example are placed in several different locations of this activity. These benchmarks are shared with students so they are aware of what is important and why.

Below is a list of possible benchmarks for this sample activity:

- Discuss key terms and definitions through a brainstorming activity centered on the world map.
- Discuss topography and climate differences, with emphasis placed on longitude and latitude and how this impacts weather.
- Identify data collected from the database in terms of specific patterns, cause and effect, stability and change within the different regions of the world.
- Outline mathematical models that can be utilized to answer questions on temperature and climate, such as *How does the height of the sun impact surface temperature?*

In each of the benchmark assessments described above, you determine if students are achieving the intended learning for each task. Use the identified benchmarks to formatively assess students to help meet their learning needs and your lesson objectives.

Figure 10.3. Establishing Benchmarks Example

IDENTIFY ESSENTIAL QUESTIONS

When examining your inquiry activity, consider the following questions to help guide the design of your instruction and identify what is important for students to understand. Essential questions are pulled from your standards, but also incorporate real-world elements. Tie topics into the bigger picture and relevant, real-world events in designing your authentic assessment.

First and most importantly, to add authenticity to the assessment, consider how students encounter the activity in the real world. You know students are thinking this very question, so it is helpful if you provide a rationale right from the beginning. For example, one of your students may ask, "Why do we always read literature that is sad?"

How do you respond? How can you connect the assessment to the real-world interests of students, aiding them in responding to this question as well as demonstrating what they learned?

Next, ask yourself what makes this unit universal in scope. In other words, how does it apply to other units and subject areas? We do not teach in isolation. All content is connected and interwoven. Try to identify ways in which your topic combines and mixes with other topics and subjects. For example, what is the connection between mathematical models as they relate to temperature and geography, history, social studies, English, science, music, or art?

In addition, topics discussed in class tend to have an underlying issue or problem, so it is important to determine what this may be in the real world. Then, find ways that you can incorporate the issue into your learning task. When you identify relevant underlying problems that students can relate to, you effect and hold their motivation and interest, especially in your assessments.

Another question to consider when designing your assessment is what would obstruct student demonstration of their understanding, especially if they just did not get it? You want to provide enough time for students to think about their learning and understanding at each stage so they are able to dig deeply and meaningfully within these identified problem areas and resolve the issues at hand, learning how to learn.

Additional or similar questions might be

- How does your assessment align with your students' interests?
- How does your assessment align with, and then extend, your learning activities to encourage students to view the problem differently while still using the skills and knowledge they learned throughout the lesson/unit?
- How can students improve in the learning task by completing an assessment?

- What types of feedback do students need to receive and by whom?
- What complex thinking is required?

IDENTIFY LEARNING ACTIVITIES

When you look at assessments in the planning stage of your activity design, focus on intended outcomes. Determine what type of evidence is needed for students to understand the important concepts of the lesson. Next, what specific responses are you looking for to determine if students understand? What determines a correct response or an incorrect response?

This is where you create a rubric (discussed below) and specific criteria to determine student learning. Does the evidence align with the goals and objectives of the unit? Are students learning what you intended?

Questions to consider when identifying your learning activities include the following:

- How will students demonstrate content proficiency?
- How will digital technology support student learning and formative assessment (e.g., feedback, knowledge, creativity, and/or performance)?
- How will digital tools help students present content proficiency?
- How can I ensure student engagement in an authentic problem-solving task that aligns with my standards?
- How will summative assessment emphasize higher order thinking?

CREATING A RUBRIC

When designing an authentic assessment, it is important to create a rubric. Otherwise, how will you determine the degree to which students met the performance task? Just like in a traditional assessment, you want to first *identify your standards*. Identify clearly what students need to know and what they need to be able to do once they complete the unit. Without this knowledge, you cannot effectively design your authentic task.

The reason to focus on the broad nature of a standard is because it is more complex in scope than your objectives. Like the unit, a standard spans beyond one class period allowing for deeper thinking to take place during the assessment itself. An objective is usually written at the level of a lesson plan and is more narrow in scope.

The next step is to *identify specific tasks* that are relevant in the world your students live in and the subject they are studying to give it authenticity.

This provides structure to help design your problem. Specific tasks are useful for scaffolding by choosing good questions, as well as various media and resources. Technology tools incorporated into the tasks help students frame their inquiry and allow them to demonstrate application of learning to solve the authentic problem chosen.

An important step when selecting a task is to look at your standards and then look to the real world to determine how it could be solved. For example, in a math class where students must be able to compute fractions, you could have them adjust the toppings on a pizza recipe or measure and buy enough paint to redo the reading area in the classroom.

After identifying the project's authentic tasks, create a rubric or scoring scale to identify criteria that determines what makes a good performance as well as identify levels of performance. Criterion communicate the expectations of each task and assist in constructing knowledge and skills needed to gain a successful outcome. Rubric criterion set the expectations that each student should demonstrate as evidence of learning.

When identifying your criterion, limit yourself to only the essential ones. This generally runs between three to ten. The more complex your task, the more criteria identified. The goal is not to assess everything in the task, but only what is critical. For example, perhaps it is not essential to provide criteria for practicing appropriate digital literacy or writing skills because it is assumed your students were already practicing these skills and have knowledge in these areas. As a result, it is expected that each assignment and assessment already demonstrates their understanding of both.

When you provide a rubric in the beginning of an activity, you allow students to see what is important about the activity. They can work toward each of the identified criterion in the rubric throughout the activity itself. The descriptions should help students design their authentic project successfully.

As you outline what is important, it is also meaningful to create a rubric as a class. This coconstruction with students allows for their ideas to be brought forward, and with your questioning, students will obtain a better understanding of what a quality performance or demonstration looks like.

Remember that rubrics are only as good as you design them. The more specific your expectations are and the more the rubric is aligned with your learning standards, the better your rubric evaluation tool.

SUMMARY

Throughout your inquiry-oriented activity, a very robust learning experience has been created for students. Experiential experiences have been tied into your learning standards and you incorporated real-world elements that ignited student interest and motivation into the process of thinking and ultimately learning.

As you identified learning standards, you also outlined objectives. Next, you defined specifically how students demonstrate understanding throughout the activity. You identified important benchmarks or places within the lesson that provide you and your students with knowledge on how they are doing at that point in the activity. For example, Are they understanding? Do they need guidance to move forward?

As benchmarks were identified, you also thought about what tasks students needed to complete to demonstrate the knowledge gained. What performances do you want them to present to confirm understanding? Throughout the activity, you ensured that both informal and formal assessments were embedded.

It is important to provide enough support for students to learn and grow in their understanding of the topics explored. In order to do this, continuous rather than summative assessments are needed. The goal of inquiry-based learning is to ensure that students understand and then are able to apply their understanding in new ways. Authentic assessments are good measures to determine this new knowledge.

With assessments, ensure that you are not waiting until the end of an activity to evaluate students but that you identify your criteria early on, share this criterion with students, and then confirm that they are on task and understanding the activity throughout.

REFLECTION

1. What is important for students to understand and be able to do as they complete the inquiry lesson? What should they know once the inquiry is complete?
2. Is the authentic assessment aligned to your problem? To your inquiry? How will students practice skills learned throughout the inquiry to demonstrate understanding?
3. What benchmarks have you identified to formatively assess student skills and knowledge—before instruction, during instruction, and after instruction? What will you do if students are not grasping what is important?
4. What will your rubric measure? How does the rubric apply to the skills and knowledge students practiced and gained through the inquiry project?
5. As you review chapter 10, add key ideas and concepts into your inquiry framework.

SKILL BUILDING ACTIVITY

This activity focuses on incorporating continuous and authentic assessments throughout your inquiry project. Revisit the inquiry-oriented activity that you have been working on and review your learning standards, goal, and essential question.

Write down four specific benchmarks you want your students to achieve. Next, determine what authentic activities will help students meet each of these benchmarks. Write down each activity, highlighting standards for each one.

Design and develop a rubric that ties your learning goal, standards, and essential question by writing specific criterion that guides your students to a successful outcome.

Ask a colleague to review and provide feedback. Important questions include

- Do you have authentic assessments that align with your intended benchmarks?
- Do you have a blend of formative assessments to inform your instructional decisions and student learning challenges?
- Are cognitive competencies, such as critical and creative thinking, being assessed?
- How have you integrated digital tools into your assessments as an authentic tool?

Chapter Eleven

Engaging Learners around Inquiry with Blended Learning

Your principal, Ms. Leeds, discussed the use of blended learning in the last faculty meeting. She underscored the importance of seeing blended learning as a way to engage students more continually in active learning around your curricular goals, even if some students did not have Internet at home. She emphasized that teaching at a distance was not a static way for students to access information or even homework from your class, but that it should be dynamic and interactive.

You and your team are somewhat perplexed about incorporating blended learning into your inquiry project and decide to look into it further. Building upon what you have created thus far as a team, identify specific ways that you can enhance student inquiry by including meaningful online tasks that students work on both within class and online at a distance?

Consider how you will plan an online activity. One that requires students to actively think about their learning and the content. An activity that requires collaboration with others to build a specific skill or understanding around a learning objective. It will be delivered online outside of regular class time and be seamlessly connected to your inquiry project.

You and your team decide to focus on the following questions:

- *How can you provide multiple representations of content in an online setting?*
- *How will your students find and use resources found online?*
- *What other technology tool(s) will students use at a distance? How do these tools align with your learning goals?*
- *How will you incorporate opportunities for students to interact with the blended learning content by thinking more critically and even creatively?*

- How will you differentiate instruction, resources, and so forth in the distance learning environment? How will you work with students who do not have Internet access at home?

Blended learning is growing in popularity within educational institutions and among teachers and students alike. Also termed e-learning or Web hybrid, it continues to evolve and take varied forms. One constant is that blended learning incorporates traditional face-to-face instruction with online, Internet-based components and digital tools.

When offering learning at a distance and teaching online, it is necessary to rethink your teaching practice. Just like you have done with the inquiry model, you must adjust pedagogical practices to incorporate more opportunity for discovery, collaboration, and active learning. Learning materials are revamped or extended so they are visible and easily accessible. Copyright issues and other ethical considerations need to be taken into account. Figure 11.1 provides an overview of blended learning.

INTERACTIVE COURSE DESIGN AND BLENDED LEARNING

Interactive course design requires students to be actively engaged with the content, whether it is participating in a simulation and then critically thinking about a process or procedure, answering questions or solving a problem while watching a video, or peer editing a wiki page. When thinking about each element in your lesson, including a blended experience, you are seeking ways for students to think about their learning while interacting with the content and one another to solve an authentic problem using real-world tools.

Digital tools have many purposes in teaching and learning. They can help organize and distribute content and resources as well as provide opportunities for students to engage with the content and with other peers, the teacher, and outside experts.

Digital tools can include a blog, Twitter, a wiki, augmented reality, or even a space in a virtual world as well as a mobile device and an app. These all provide a medium that allows students to access resources and information in a variety of formats, such as video, audio, primary sources, and hyperlinked text. Students can also use these digital tools to create resources that can be shared with others to demonstrate and extend knowledge gained.

Extending and enhancing opportunities for students to spend more quality time with course content is the goal of blended learning. Learning at a distance in a blended learning format provides an additional avenue, and

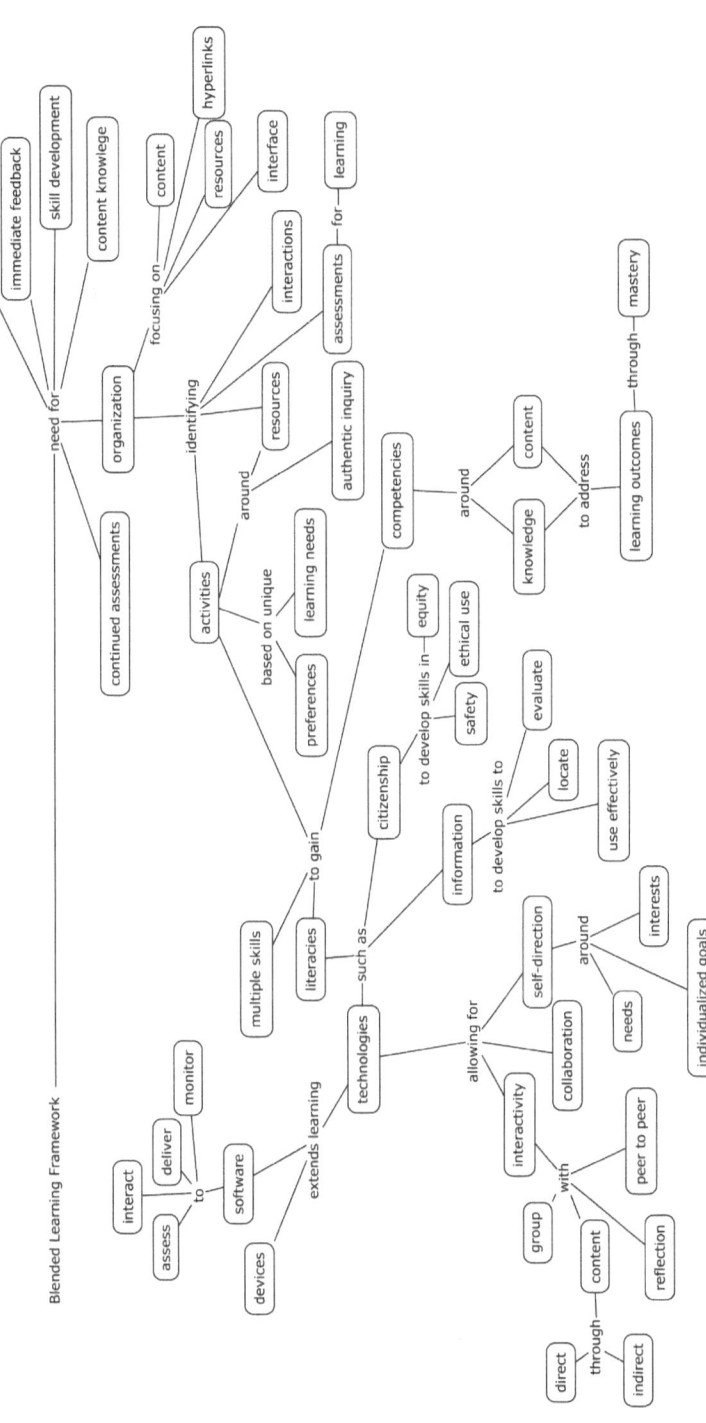

Figure 11.1. Blended Learning Framework

potentially a more systematic opportunity, to meet student needs by providing the following attributes:

- Greater flexibility in learning times and ways to access a problem or issue
- Varied methods to present information using additional teaching strategies and online resources
- Additional time to collaborate with others outside of the traditional classroom
- Opportunities to continuously assess learning

Rich and dynamic resources, organized and scaffolded content, built-in interactivity, ample opportunities for collaboration and cooperation with both the teacher and other students, and timely feedback and reflection are all critical and necessary components for a successful blended learning course.

While online or distance learning is typically defined as 100 percent Web-based instruction, blended learning incorporates a mix of online learning with face-to-face instruction. Blended learning generally has between 30 and 70 percent of course content offered online. Consider how blended learning can be used to enhance your classroom instruction and increase meaningful learning. More contact time with the curriculum content is provided at a distance and in a way that is not considered just "homework."

As the example in figure 11.2 illustrates, a well-designed blended learning experience should engage students in the problem being solved and increase quality time spent on the overall task. Research suggests that there is a direct relationship to increasing student time-on-task and overall learning. When designing instruction for a blended approach to teaching and learning, consider ways you can complement both online and face-to-face instructional approaches.

INSTRUCTIONAL DESIGN FOR THE BLENDED LEARNING CLASSROOM

The use of technology in a blended learning classroom is paramount. When considering the integration of technology and instruction, start with your teaching goal and learning outcome rather than the technology tool. Once you have a grasp on what students need to accomplish, then think about how or if a technology tool will help achieve that goal successfully.

As with any new learning environment, try to anticipate the learning curve students experience with blended learning or using a Web-enhanced instructional delivery. To help students be successful and effective, provide them

> In a blended language arts course, an inquiry lesson has been designed around the following question:
>
> *How have music and poetry connected us to our past and present?*
>
> A full day of in-class activities has been planned by the teacher, but the above question is elicited beforehand so students enter class already thinking about it and are better prepared.
>
> Primary source data from the Library of Congress and other resources is provided in class that highlights different time periods of music and poetry and breaks them down by themes, such as rhyme, melody, voice, audience, and symbol.
>
> Students are divided into small groups around these five themes and each student team is assigned a theme and time period.
>
> There is a face-to-face class discussion where common themes are pulled together for further research, debate, and analysis.
>
> Following class, students access a Web resource online that was created by the teacher. Just like in class, it is organized around the theme and time period.
>
> Under each theme is an introductory paragraph to hook (or motivate) and inform students of the task to be completed online with some guiding questions. Additionally, primary source data such as images, podcasts of songs, lyrics, poetry, and even letters written by the artists are included within the website.
>
> Students are tasked to research the question posed for the inquiry lesson at a distance and are motivated to present their findings to their individual group members as well as the class as a whole in the next face-to-face class meeting.

Figure 11.2. Blended Learning Example

with sufficient time within the course to become familiar with the material, both online and face-to-face. Encourage them to ask questions both to you and each other.

Provide information in a variety of entrance points just in case there is a problem with technology and access. Whether you provide in-class time to introduce the online activity and help students get started, send the content to their cell phone, or provide a flash drive with instructions on how to access the course at a distance and outside of class, seek ways to ensure students are successful.

Scaffolding and "chunking" information can also help students understand the material and how it is presented. Provide online assistants or avatars. Even short video segments inserted throughout the online portion of the course can guide students with specific instructions to build skills or provide helpful information to keep them focused on the learning task.

Sequencing is also key in a blended environment. Plan how students should most effectively move through the content, progressing and building on their overall knowledge. Provide a clear outline that advances students through the learning objectives indicating how the resources and each learning activity aligns to the learning goal.

By scaffolding and sequencing the content for learners, you provide small but meaningful amounts of information. This coupled with planned interactive experiences around the inquiry activity encourages students to stay focused and interested throughout the blended learning process.

Figure 11.3 provides guidelines for blended learning lesson design. Each point focuses on designing engaging and active learning experiences using authentic resources and tools that complement your learning goals. By using this multilayered approach when designing instruction both inside the

---

1. Incorporate resources that include multiple perspectives and representations for concepts studied.
2. Utilize course design (navigation, organization, images, hyperlinks), digital tools, and resources to encourage students to reflect, regulate learning, and think more deeply about the material.
3. Provide opportunities for students to take greater control of their own learning process, such as identifying learning goals and objectives.
4. Ensure that your authentic problem is guiding student inquiry and aligns with intended learning outcomes.
5. Encourage active thinking around primary sources to help students develop complex thinking and to complement the authenticity of the problem.
6. Ensure that new knowledge construction is at the center of each activity so there is minimal reproduction of information.
7. Consider the previous knowledge, beliefs, and attitudes of students (mental models) when designing activities and including resources and materials.
8. Ensure that problem solving, higher order thinking, and deep understanding are at the center of each activity.
9. Allow opportunities for exploration to be incorporated in the form of questions to encourage students to seek knowledge independently as well as collectively to manage pursuit of their goals.
10. Include apprenticeship learning with the goal of increasing opportunities for task experience, skill development, and knowledge acquisition.
11. Find ways to incorporate interdisciplinary learning into your blended and online environment so complexity of thought is amplified.
12. Show students firsthand alternative viewpoints by enforcing collaborative and cooperative learning.
13. Scaffold to help students perform just beyond the limits of their abilities.
14. Incorporate as many authentic assessments throughout the activity as possible to encourage reflection and thought about the instructional content.

Figure 11.3. Blended Learning Guidelines

classroom and online, you are developing and strengthening student skills as well as providing active ways to engage in practicing complex thinking and problem solving.

USING BLOOM'S TAXONOMY IN BLENDED LEARNING

Introduced in chapter 4 in terms of applying technology integration, Bloom's Taxonomy can also be incorporated into your blended lesson design. Originally developed in 1956 and updated in 2001, Bloom's Taxonomy can be applied to instructional design to guide student learning along a thinking continuum. When coupled with blended learning, your inquiry activities can be developed to highlight both active and engaged learning within class and online.

Within the taxonomy, there are six cognitive levels and these move from lower to higher order thinking. As a review, the six levels are listed here:

1. Remembering (knowledge)
2. Understanding (comprehension)
3. Applying
4. Analyzing
5. Evaluating
6. Creating (synthesizing)

These six levels provide opportunities to develop both foundational skills as well as more advanced skills that are needed when applying what is learned.

When designing activities that encourage thinking around authentic problems, students need to apply what they learned by asking questions and seeking good resources and information to answer those questions. Blended learning helps to set the stage for deeper investigation, which then includes analysis, evaluation, and synthesis.

As you think about creating learning activities within your blended environment, do so in a way that enhances the in-class portion of the activity. For example:

- What will stimulate student interest both in class and online?
- How can students think more critically about a topic, idea, or event in the blended learning format?
- How can students extend what they have learned through blended learning?
- How can they be more actively involved during the in-class activity with work done previously online?

MAKING BLENDED LEARNING ACCESSIBLE

When incorporating blended learning, consider the digital tools that will be included from beginning to the end of the activity. Your goal is for information to be accessible by presenting information in multiple formats. Students should be able to reflect on their learning and interact with the content and others in the class in multiple ways. Additional considerations include digital literacy and online safety. Scaffold student learning experiences for preparation at each stage of the process.

As you design blended activities, consider how to organize information. Think about chunking content around themes and resources. What types of activities are needed to engage your learners? How can technology help students access content in more engaged ways? How can technology assist in students demonstrating what they learned as they are learning it?

Collaboration, community, and active learning are important to consider in your design. The goal is not to create a video post in your course management system for students to view at home passively and complete a worksheet, but instead to create interactive learning opportunities that engage students around what they are learning and the world around them by asking good questions and then having them think more deeply by researching, applying, analyzing, evaluating, and even creating. Figure 11.4 shows numerous ways to present content online.

When incorporating an inquiry-based approach, digital tools such as multimedia, as well as analysis, collaboration, and communication tools can be incorporated to allow students the opportunity to explore and interact with one another and the content in complex yet seamless ways.

When thinking about presenting content, students should use an active approach throughout your inquiry. Find ways where students can actively engage with the content and one another through questioning and manipulating.

When integrating media, for example, have students interact with the media or the message by doing something meaningful—not just passively watching. Move beyond worksheets and begin having students think by constructing concept maps, cartoons, manipulating data on a spreadsheet, or even compiling new information to design a video.

Constantly seek ways for students to engage with the content, one another, and their own thinking. Allow them to question what they are learning and why they are learning it. Challenge them to think differently and to take ownership throughout the learning process.

For example, if you create a video to introduce your activity and content, make it short and stop the video often to have students do something, such as taking notes at specific points. This could be done on the class concept map

Ways to Present Online Content	
Representation of Information	videos
	audio recordings
	slide shows
	text in various reading levels
	variety of support resources
	translations
	graphic representations, such as diagrams, images, and illustrations
Expression of Understanding	written reports
	audio presentations
	maps
	diagrams
	videos
	slide shows
	graphs
	concept maps
	outlines
	hands-on activities
	blogs
	wikis
	shared writing or editing
Student Engagement	role playing
	interviewing experts
	participating in threaded discussions
	brainstorming
	working in teams
	conducting experiments
	playing games
	getting involved in the community

Figure 11.4. Presenting Online Content

where each member of the class sees what other classmates are thinking. Or possibly, with each pause of the video, have students work through a problem in order to practice what they are learning. Then, have students create a cartoon that they present on the class blog for discussion and debate.

Find multiple ways to present information to students. Other examples include showing a video from TED Talks. There are also a variety of primary sources or even popular news stories, personal blogs, virtual labs, and games that can help get students thinking about your content.

As you design your blended learning experience, additionally consider ways students can work collaboratively, such as asking questions, peer editing, storing and sharing documents or resources, or organizing and solving a problem as a group.

SUMMARY

This chapter provides an overview on incorporating blended learning into an inquiry lesson. It examines the idea that blended learning can be integrated into instruction as an active learning process centered around a thinking curriculum. A blended learning approach can help provide different and further engagement for students to access content and actively participate with one another while doing so.

As you think about incorporating blended learning into your teaching, consider how you can further engage students to work directly with one another and the content by integrating meaningful connections between curricular goals, student learning goals, and digital technology, all while making it interactive.

REFLECTION

1. How can you incorporate blended learning into your instruction to engage students to think more deeply about your authentic problem?
2. What digital tools can you integrate at each stage of your activity to encourage students to access, explore, and interact with the content and one another?
3. How will you use Bloom's Taxonomy in your blended activity to help develop a more complex task that requires complex thinking?
4. What barriers, real or perceived, can you identify concerning the implementation of blended learning into your inquiry unit? Identify solutions and ways around these barriers.
5. How would you respond to the scenario presented at the beginning of this chapter?

SKILL BUILDING ACTIVITY

In this chapter, blended learning was investigated. Think about how blended learning can be integrated into your inquiry lesson to engage students to interact with your intended learning goals and one another at deeper levels so that they can then share what they learned in a meaningful way.

As you think about your activity, incorporate the following elements:

- Establish a connection to your authentic problem guiding student inquiry.
- Provide a guiding question to hook your students, encouraging them to dig deeper and be motivated to complete the blended learning portion of the activity.
- Provide multiple representations of content in an online setting.
- Use Bloom's Taxonomy to engage students to understand, think, and then create.
- Integrate multiple ways students can demonstrate understanding.
- Incorporate digital tools that present information, allow students to interact with and think about information, and can be used by students to communicate, collaborate, and share understanding.
- Identify how your online blended format complements your face-to-face portion of your activity.

References

CHAPTER 1. TEACHING WITH INQUIRY: AN INTRODUCTION

Ferriter. W. (2014, January 28). Should we be engaging or empowering learners? The Tempered Radical Blog.

Michael Lawrence Films. (1990). "Steve Jobs." *Memory and Imagination: New pathways to the Library of Congress*.

National Education Association. (2014). *Preparing 21st century students for a global society: An educator's guide to the "Four Cs."* Washington, DC: National Education Association.

Pi-Hsia, H., Gwo-Jen, H., Yueh-Hsun, L., Tsung-Hsun, W., Vogel, B., Milrad, M., and Johansson, E. (2014). A problem-based ubiquitous learning approach to improving the questioning abilities of elementary school students. *Journal of Educational Technology and Society, 17*(4), 316–334.

Rosefsky Saavedra, A., and Opfer, V. D. (2012). Learning 21st-century skills requires 21st century teaching. *Phi Delta Kappan, 94*(2), 8–13.

Treffinger, D. (2008). Preparing creative and critical thinkers. *Educational Leadership, 65*.

US Department of Education. *Effects of technology on the classroom and students.* Available at Office of Educational Research and Improvement, US Department of Education. SRI International.

Vockley, M. (2007). *Maximizing the impact: The pivotal role of technology in a 21st century education system.* Eugene, OR: International Society for Technology in Education; Glen Burnie, MD: State Educational Technology Directors Association; Tucson, AZ: Partnership for 21st Century Skills.

CHAPTER 2. TEACHING AND STUDENT LEARNING USING INQUIRY

Barell, J. F. (2007). *Why are school buses always yellow: Teaching for inquiry preK–5.* Thousand Oaks, CA: Corwin Press.

Bransford, J., Brown, A., and Cocking, R. (Eds.). (1999). *How people learn.* National Research Council. Washington, DC: National Academy Press.

Herron, M. D. (1971). The nature of scientific enquiry. *The School Review, 79*(2), 171–212.

Jacobs, H. H. (2010). *Curriculum 21: Essential education for a changing world.* Alexandria, VA: Association for Supervision and Curriculum Development.

Reiser, B. J. (2004). Scaffolding complex learning: The mechanisms of structuring and problematizing student work. *Journal of the Learning Sciences, 13,* 273–304.

Resnick. L., and Klopfer, L. E. (1989). Toward the thinking curriculum: An overview. In L. Resnick and L. E. Klopfer (Eds.), *Toward the thinking curriculum: Current cognitive research.* Alexandria, VA: Association for Supervision and Curriculum Development.

CHAPTER 3. INTEGRATING COMPUTER TECHNOLOGIES AS A COGNITIVE TOOL

Christensen, C. M., Horn, M. B., and Johnson, C. W. (2008). *Disrupting class: How disruptive innovation will change the way the world learns.* New York: McGraw-Hill.

Jonassen, D. H., and Reeves, T. C. (1996). Learning with technology: Using computers as cognitive tools. In D. H. Jonassen (Ed.), *Handbook of research for educational communications and technology* (pp. 693–719). New York: Macmillan.

Learning Point Associates/NCREL. (2005). *Critical issue: Using technology to improve student achievement.* Naperville, IL: Learning Point Associates/The North Central Regional Educational Laboratory (NCREL).

Papert, S. (1993). *Mindstorms: Children, computers, and powerful ideas* (second edition). New York: Basics Books.

Perkins, D. N. (1986). *Knowledge as design.* Hillsdale, NJ: Lawrence Erlbaum Associates.

CHAPTER 4. TECHNOLOGY INTEGRATION MODELS

Anderson, L. W., Krathwohl, D. R., Airasian, P. W., Cruikshank, K. A., Mayer, R. E., Pintrich, P. R., . . . Wittrock, M. C. (2000). *A taxonomy for learning, teaching, and assessing: A revision of Bloom's taxonomy of educational objectives.* Upper Saddle River, NJ: Pearson.

Bloom's digital taxonomy. (n.d.). CommonSenseMedia.org.
Candice, M. (n.d.). SAMR in 120 Seconds. YouTube video.
Christie, Alice. (2011). Dr. Alice Christie's GoogleTreks.org.
Harris, J., and Hofer, M. (n.d.). Learning Activity Types website. Williamsburg, VA: School of Education, College of William and Mary.
Jackson, R. R. (2009). Know where your students are going. In *Never work harder than your students and other principles of great teaching*. Alexandria, VA: Association for Supervision and Curriculum Development.
Koehler, M. J., and Mishra, P. (2009). What is technological pedagogical content knowledge? *Contemporary Issues in Technology and Teacher Education, 9*(1), 60–70.
National Educational Technology Standards for Students (NETs). International Society for Technology in Education (ISTE). ISTE.org.
Shulman, L. S. (1986). Those who understand: Knowledge growth in teaching. *Educational Researcher, 15*(2), 4–14.
Substitution, Augmentation, Modification, Redefinition (SAMR) model. (n.d.). Developed by Ruben Puentedura. Hippasus.com.
Technology Integration Matrix (TIM). (2016). Florida Center for Instructional Technology, College of Education, University of South Florida.
Technology Pedagogy and Content Knowledge (TPACK) framework. (n.d.). Matthew J. Koehler, editor, College of Education, Michigan State University.

CHAPTER 5. SOCIAL MEDIA AND COLLABORATION

Bringing acceptable-use policies into the 21st century. (2012). Education World.com.
Communication and collaboration. (n.d.). Partnership for 21st century learning (P21.org).
Davis, V. (2015, February 19). A guidebook to social media in the classroom. Edutopia.org.
Green, H., and Hannon, C. (2007). Their space: Education for a digital generation. Demos.co.uk.
Hargadon, S. (2016). Classroom 2.0 Web community (classroom20.com).
Jordan, B. (2012). A teacher's guide to using social media and the Internet in the classroom. ReallyGoodStuff.com.
Seth Godin on social networking. (2009). YouTube video.
Shirky, C. (2012, September 25). How the Internet will (one day) transform government. TED Talk video.
Shirky, C. (2009, June 15). How social media can make history. TED Talk video.
Social networking. (n.d.). Pew Research Center (pewresearch.org).
Social networking explained. (2016). CommonCraft.com.
Tolisano, S. R. (2009, November 19). Backchanneling with elementary school students. Langwitches weblog.

CHAPTER 6. DIGITAL CITIZENSHIP

6 ways to make PowerPoint more engaging and interactive. (2014, October 28). DiscoveryEducation.com.

Cutler, D. (2015, October 22). Modeling constructive online behavior. Edutopia.org.

Davis, V. (2014, October). What your students really need to know about digital citizenship. Edutopia.org.

Digital citizenship. (2016). Edutopia.org.

Digital citizenship for teachers. (2013). Video Playlist. Teaching Channel.org.

Digital compliance and student privacy: A roadmap for schools. (2016). iKeepSafe.org.

Educating digital citizens. (n.d.). Video Playlist. TeachingChannel.org.

Hicks, K. (2015, July 9). A teacher's guide to digital citizenship. Edudemic.com.

How to make great presentations with Pecha Kucha. (n.d.). GlobalDigitalCitizen Foundation.org.

K–12 digital citizenship curriculum. (n.d.). CommonSenseMedia.org.

Miller, A. (2013, February 21). Ideas for digital citizenship PBL projects. Edutopia.org.

Ribble, M. (2008). Passport to digital citizenship: A journey toward appropriate technology use at school and at home. *Learning and Leading with Technology, 36*(4), 14–17.

The art of concise presentations. (n.d.). Pecha Kucha 20×20 (pechakucha.org).

The Lessig method of presentation. (2005). PresentationZen.com.

CHAPTER 7. INFORMATION LITERACY

Information literacy competency standards for higher education. (2016). American LibraryAssociation.org.

Kathy Schrock's critical evaluation surveys. (2016, September 30). Kathy Schrock's Guide to Everything (schrockguide.net).

Nolan, M. (2012, Fall). How to separate fact and fiction online. TED Talk video.

November, A. (1998). *Teaching Zack to think.* NovemberLearning.com. Posted February 27, 2012.

Standards for the 21st century learner. (2016). AmericanLibraryAssociation.org.

Teacher tap: Evaluating Internet resources. (2013). Eduscapes.com.

CHAPTER 8. ENGAGING IN PROBLEM-BASED LEARNING

Barrett, T. (2010). The problem-based learning process as finding and being in flow. *Innovations in Education and Teaching International, 47*(2), 165–174.

BIE tools—PBL project search. (n.d.). BuckInstituteforEducation.org.

Difference between projects and project-based learning. (2016). TeachThought.com.
Larmer, J., and Mergendoller, J. R. (2010, September). Seven essentials for project-based learning. *Educational Leadership, 68*(1), 34–37.
Project-based learning. (2016). Edutopia.org.

CHAPTER 9. GLOBAL CONNECTIONS AND TELECOLLABORATIVE LEARNING

Harris, J. (2001, May). Teachers as telecollaborative project designers: A curriculum-based approach. *Contemporary Issues in Technology and Teacher Education, 1*(3), 429–442.
Harris, J. (2000). Taboo topic no longer: Why telecollaborative projects sometimes fail. *Learning and Leading with Technology, 27*(5), 58–61.
Silva, P. U., Meagher, M. E., Valenzuela, M., and Crenshaw, S. (1996, February). Email: Real-life classroom experiences with foreign languages. *Learning and Leading with Technology, 23*(5), 10–12.

CHAPTER 10. USING TECHNOLOGIES FOR ASSESSMENT AND FEEDBACK

Brookhart, S. M. (2013). What are rubrics and why are they important? In *How to Create and Use Rubrics for Formative Assessment and Grading* (pp. 3–14). Alexandria, VA: Association for Supervision and Curriculum Development.
Paris, S. G., and Winograd, P. (1990). How metacognition can promote academic learning and instruction. In B. F. Jones and L. Idol (Eds.), *Dimensions of Thinking and Cognitive Instruction* (pp. 15–51). Hillsdale: NJ. Lawrence Erlbaum Associates.
Pellegrino, J. W., and Hilton, M. L. (2013). *Education for life and work: Developing transferable knowledge and skills in the 21st century*. Washington, DC: National Academies Press.
Wiggins, G. (1998). Ensuring authentic performance. In *Educative assessment: Designing assessments to inform and improve student performance* (pp. 21–42). San Francisco: Jossey-Bass.

CHAPTER 11. ENGAGING LEARNERS AROUND INQUIRY WITH BLENDED LEARNING

AlDahdouh, A. A., Osório, A. J., and Caires, S. (2015, October). Understanding knowledge network, learning and connectivism. *International Journal of Instructional Technology and Distance Learning, 12*(10), 3–24.

Bloom, B. (1984). *Taxonomy of educational objectives*. Boston, MA: Allyn and Bacon.

Brindley, J. E., Walti, C., and Blaschke, L. M. (2009). Creating effective collaborative learning groups in an online environment. *The International Review in Research in Open and Distance Learning, 10*(3), 1–18.

Core Rules of Netiquette. (2011). Excerpted from *Netiquette* by Virginia Shea. Albion.com.

Creative Commons Licenses. (n.d.). CreativeCommons.org.

Gagne, R., Briggs, L., and Wager, W. (1992). *Principles of instructional design* (fourth edition). Fort Worth, TX: HBJ College Publishers.

International Association for K–12 Online Learning. (2016). iNACOL.org.

Krathwohl, D. R. (2002, Autumn). A revision of Bloom's taxonomy: An overview. *Theory into Practice, 41*(4), 212–218.

Multimedia Educational Resource for Learning and Online Teaching. (2016). Merlot.org.

National Center on Universal Design for Learning. (2015). UDLCenter.org.

OnlineLearningConsortium.org (2016).

OpenEducationalResourcesCommons.org (2016).

Revised Bloom's taxonomy. (2016). Iowa State University Center for Excellence in Learning and Teaching (CELT.iastate.edu).

About the Author

Dr. Teresa Coffman is a professor of education in the Department of Curriculum and Instruction at the University of Mary Washington in Fredericksburg, Virginia. She is an innovative educator and has been featured in articles on technology integration. She received the Innovative Educator of the Year Award through the Virginia Society for Technology in Education in 2014. She served as a Google Glass Explorer and continues to be at the forefront of mobile learning and wearable technologies. An accomplished presenter, Coffman has also published numerous articles and chapters in books on teaching and learning, distance education, and technology integration. This is her third book. Her master's and doctoral degrees are both in education with a specialization in instructional technology. She's available by e-mail (tcoffman@umw.edu) or Twitter (@teresacoffman).

www.ingramcontent.com/pod-product-compliance
Lightning Source LLC
Chambersburg PA
CBHW020748230426

43665CB00009B/533